Practical Internet Law for Business

For a recent list of titles in the *Artech House Telecommunications Library*,
turn to the back of this book.

Practical Internet Law for Business

Kurt M. Saunders

Artech House
Boston • London
www.artechhouse.com

Library of Congress Cataloging-in-Publication Data
Saunders, Kurt M.
Practical internet law for business / Kurt M. Saunders.
p. cm.—(Artech House telecommunications library)
Includes bibliographical references and index.
ISBN 1-58053-003-6 (alk. paper)
1. Internet—Law and legislation—United States. 2. Computer networks—Law and legislation—United States. 3. Business law—United States.
I. Title. II. Artech House telecommunications library.
KF390.5.C6 S26 2001
343.7309'944—dc21 2001035911

British Library Cataloguing in Publication Data
Saunders, Kurt M.
Practical Internet law for business. —(Artech House telecommunications library)
1. Internet—Law and legislation 2. Business law
I. Title
343' .0999
ISBN 1-58053-003-6

Cover design by Yekaterina Ratner

685 Canton Street
Norwood, MA 02062

International Standard Book Number: 1-58053-003-6
Library of Congress Catalog Card Number: 2001035911

10 9 8 7 6 5 4 3 2 1

To my mother and father, Stephanida and James

Contents

Preface

At first thought, a printed book on Internet law seems to be a bit of a contradiction in terms. After all, the Internet is the invention that launched all of us into cyberspace—a virtual place where we can now chat, socialize, shop, sell, and search for information or jobs or just about anything else we can possibly imagine. The Internet as a tool of communication and a channel of distribution has become fully integrated into our lives and our economy. Nevertheless, we also live and do business in the real world, and our on-line actions have real-world consequences. Some of these consequences involve legal risk and potential liability. No matter how far we venture into cyberspace, we remain tethered to the reality of the law. It is for this reason, and for those who work and do business in the on-line environment, that this book was written.

This book does not intend and does not promise to transform its readers into Internet law experts. If the reader's legal rights are at issue, he or she should seek the advice of a qualified and informed attorney with experience in Internet law. However, this book can serve as a reference for allowing business and systems managers, as well as entrepreneurs, to recognize and better understand the legal issues that can arise in electronic commerce. These issues span areas of law ranging from jurisdiction and criminal law to intellectual property rights and on-line privacy and security. Likewise, by understanding the legal issues that confront a business on the Internet, readers can manage or avoid the legal risks posed and succeed in his or her business objectives.

Fundamental changes in technology and society have been closely followed by significant developments in the law. This fascinating area of law, like information technology itself, is one of rapid and often unexpected change. For these reasons, it has been an honor and a challenge to write this book. I urge you to make full use of the opportunities and abilities afforded by the Internet in your lives and businesses. I welcome your ideas, comments, and suggestions for improving this work as well.

Acknowledgments

Many have contributed to the successful completion of this work. My thanks to Artech House for the opportunity to write this book and to the many members of the Artech team for their patience, hard work, and invaluable editorial suggestions. In particular, I wish to thank Barbara Lovenvirth, Mark Walsh, and John Wyzalek for their advice and guidance throughout this project. I am also indebted to my friends and to my colleagues at California State University, Northridge, for their encouragement when the enormity of this effort seemed overwhelming, and to my students, who sometimes allow me to see the trees through the forest.

1

The development and role of the Internet

It is hard to imagine that as recently as 1990, few people had heard of the Internet or imagined that such a thing as "e-commerce" would be the engine of worldwide economic growth and cultural transformation. The Internet—and information technology more generally—has affected almost every aspect of society. At the same time, the law has had to adapt to address the many novel issues that the emergence of the Internet has fueled. Familiar issues, such as property rights, privacy, and crime, are confronting businesses in unfamiliar ways, challenging some of our basic assumptions about how law and business operate. In some instances, the courts have shaped traditional legal standards to fit these challenges. In other cases, legislative bodies have stepped in to fashion brand new laws to address the situation.

Regardless of the line of commerce pursued, a firm that employs computers in its operations or that engages in commercial transactions on-line must be aware of the legal issues that will arise in the contemporary business environment. Ultimately, this is the purpose of this book. As an introduction to the legal issues discussed, this chapter begins by providing a brief historical overview of the development of the Internet and then outlines some of the most important legal issues facing Internet businesses.

What is the Internet?

The Internet is an enormous network that interconnects numerous smaller groups of interlinked computer networks. A computer network is a group of computers linked to one another so that they can share files and exchange messages. A computer network is connected to other networks, which are in turn connected to other networks, and allow each computer in any network to communicate with computers on any other network in the system. As such, the Internet is a network of networks that links people, institutions, businesses, and governments around the world in a decentralized medium of international communications. All of the interconnected networks share information using various common data transfer protocols, which are previously agreed-upon methods of communications to interchange information. No single government or institution administers the Internet, and there is no centralized storage location, control center, or communications channel for the Internet.

Describing the entire history of computing and the innumerable technical aspects of the Internet are beyond the scope of this book, [1] but it is useful to have a general understanding of the nature of the Internet and how it operates before moving on to discuss the legal issues that confront it. To that end, Professor Gregory Rawlins uses the highly effective metaphor of a giant, imaginary building to describe, in a nontechnical way, how the Internet works:

> [I]magine that [the Internet] is a giant building where you can instantly teleport yourself from room to room on a whim. There is, as yet, no notion of its distances, location, or scale. In this imaginary building the size of London, every two of the people in the building could talk to each other if they wished. The city-sized building is divided into wings, the wings into floors, and each floor into millions of rooms. Some of the rooms have a big blackboard that anyone can scribble anything on. The posted information can be a written message, an image, a movie, a whale song, a conversation—anything. Anyone looking into such a conference room can see everything on its blackboard.
>
> In other rooms of the giant communication building, groups of people

you can't see—and who can't see you (at least today)—are chatting. They're all madly scribbling on the same blackboard at the same time, each one in a separate little area. They can all see what everyone else is cribbling, so it's a kind of ongoing written conversation—a visible chat.

In thousands of other rooms, people are playing very specialized games, writing a kind of continuing, do-it-yourself novel. Each person is a character, or more than one character, in a fantasy world conjured into existence by the words of all the other participants. They're having an experience—a very addictive experience.

Still other rooms are sites of town meetings. The residents of these towns may have never met physically and may live all over the world. But they are all passionately interested in a certain topic—perhaps gun control, tea drinking, computer crime, recycling, or white supremacy. The list of topics goes on and on. From bondage to beauty queens, from Tibetan ashrams to drug abuse, from action films to Japanese haikus—whatever your kink, on the net you'll find thousands, perhaps millions of others who share it.

Some of those following a discussion never contribute anything to it, and many net denizens follow numerous discussions. People can create new discussion rooms if they want to, once they find others to talk to. If they wish, they can make their conferences private, so that outsiders have to be initiated to be let in.

Everyone on the net also has a private lockable room. Inside it you can have complete privacy if you wish, although it has a pneumatic tube others can use to send you messages. Those messages might be anything—a brief note, a video conference call, a movie excerpt. You can choose to read the messages, destroy them, edit them, save them, repost them, or do whatever else you wish with them. You can send mail to yourself, to a specific person or group, or to one or more of the blackboards in the building. On the door of your room you can also post information you want browsers to read. Such messages can be of any length—even whole encyclopedias' worth—and they can be so interesting that hundreds of thousands of people, instead of joining the various conversations going on around the building, simply roam the corridors, teleporting themselves from door to door and reading the information posted there.

Thousands of rooms aren't owned by people at all but are used by governments and corporations. AT&T is there, as are the White House, Fuji Electric, many high schools, museums, and libraries—even some vend-

> ing machines. Their doors, like yours, display information they want the world to read. In all, there are millions of rooms in the city-sized building and, like everything else about the net, their number is doubling every few months.
>
> ...The net is a coffeehouse the size of Wyoming. And as in a coffeehouse, no one is in charge on the net. Rank, appearance, and social standing in the outside world mean nothing there unless they help guarantee someone's knowledge. Denizens of this vast building work at their own pace, choosing the size and timing of their postings and replies or simply sitting back and reading. Those who only read are there for amusement, or information, or bonding. Those who post messages are there for the same things, or for self-display, prestige, friendship, or an argument [2].

Since its creation, the Internet has functioned as a tool of collaboration among cooperating users. The following section provides an overview of the inception, creation, and growth of the Internet.

The development of the Internet

The genesis of the Internet was the Soviet Union's launch of *Sputnik* in 1957. In response, the United States formed the Advanced Research Projects Agency (ARPA) within the Department of Defense with the purpose of reestablishing the United States' lead in dual-use science and technology. ARPA commissioned the RAND Corporation to develop a plan by which the U.S. military could successfully continue to communicate during and in the aftermath of a nuclear strike. In such an event, it would be imperative to maintain communications between the president and Congress, federal agencies, and the armed forces, as well as communication links between military installations, states, and cities. Single-wire communication links would be hard to protect from attack and would be worthless if the communications command center was destroyed. Thus, the vulnerability of the communications system after a nuclear attack would lead to data loss and unreliable transmissions.

Therefore, the RAND Corporation concluded that a reliable communications network would need to have no control authority or communications command center and multiple links between any two points, and would have to assume that some data would be lost in each transmission.

This led to the development of the concept of packet switching. In packet switching, all the data sent by a computer is broken up into pieces, with each piece containing the address of origin and destination. This allows pieces of data from many different sources to commingle on the same lines, and be sorted and directed to different routes by other computers along the route. In 1962, Paul Baran of RAND released a paper entitled, "On the Distributed Communications Networks," which proposed a packet-switching network as the solution for the problem posed by ARPA. His paper described the following:

- All communications points, or nodes, in the network would be equal in status to all other points so that there would be no central authority or communications command center.
- All nodes would be connected to all other nodes, thereby forming a web of communication links, or network.
- All data transmitted would be divided into numerous smaller pieces, or packets, before being sent out onto the network.
- Each packet would be separately addressed and contain a sequence number for reassembly at the destination node.
- The packets would send back a confirmation to the transmission node to verify that the transmission to the destination node was successful.
- If no confirmation were received for a packet, the packet would be retransmitted.

The first design paper outlining a packet-switching network was published in 1967 by Lawrence Roberts. A communication sent over this network could travel any of a number of routes to its destination. Thus, a message sent from a computer in New York to a computer in Los Angeles might first be sent to a computer in Washington, then be forwarded to a computer in Pittsburgh, and then to Seattle, before finally reaching Los Angeles. If the message could not travel along that path for any reason, the message would automatically be rerouted. The network would employ packet switching by subdividing individual messages into smaller packets that would be sent independently to the destination, and then automatically reassembled by the receiving computer. While all packets of a given message might travel along the same path to the destination, if computers along the route became overloaded, then packets could be rerouted to less loaded computers.

The network was to be named the Advanced Research Projects Agency Network (ARPANET), and in 1968, the National Physical Laboratory in the United Kingdom set up the first test network consisting of several computers in a laboratory that had been connected together. The test was successful, and the first node of the network was installed at the University of California at Los Angeles in 1969. Three more nodes were added at Stanford University, the University of California at Santa Barbara, and the University of Utah. By 1971, ARPANET consisted of 15 nodes, which grew to 37 in 1972. International connections to ARPANET were added in 1973 with nodes at University College of London and the Royal Radar Establishment of Norway.

In 1973, the United States Defense Advanced Research Projects Agency (DARPA) initiated a research program to investigate techniques and technologies for interlinking packet networks of various kinds. The objective was to develop communication protocols that would allow networked computers to communicate transparently across multiple, linked packet networks. This was called the "internetting" project, and the system of networks that emerged from the research was known as the Internet. The system of protocols that was developed over the course of this research effort became known as the TCP/IP protocol suite, after the two initial protocols developed: transmission control protocol (TCP) and Internet protocol (IP). In 1975, control of ARPANET, which was by now a fully operational network, was transferred to the United States Defense Communications Agency.

The utility of a packet-switching network for education and research led ARPANET, the University of Wisconsin, and the National Science Foundation to take the initiative to establish a Computer Science Network (CSNET) in 1981, which provided networking capabilities to universities and scientists that did not have access to ARPANET. In 1983, ARPANET was split to create MILNET, which was integrated into the Defense Data Network for military applications while ARPANET continued to link those universities and commercial research facilities that did military-related research.

By 1986, the National Science Foundation (NSF) had initiated the development of its own high-speed packet-switching network, NSFNET, which today provides a major backbone communication service for the Internet. With its 45-Mbps facilities, the NSFNET carries on the order of 12 billion packets per month between the networks it links. The National Aeronautics and Space Administration (NASA) and the United States Department of Energy contributed additional backbone facilities in the form of the NSINET and ESNET, respectively. In Europe, major international backbones such as NORDUNET and others provide connectivity to more than 100,000 computers on a large number of networks. Commercial network providers in the United States and Europe are beginning to offer Internet backbone and access support on a competitive basis to any interested parties.

Regional support for the Internet is provided by various consortium networks, and local support is provided through each of the research and educational institutions. Within the United States, much of this support has come from the federal and state governments, but a considerable contribution has been made by industry. In Europe and elsewhere, support arises from cooperative international efforts and through national research organizations. During the course of its evolution, particularly after 1989, the Internet system began to integrate support for other protocol suites into its basic networking fabric. The present emphasis in the system is on multiprotocol interworking, and in particular, with the integration of the open systems interconnection (OSI) protocols into the architecture.

Both public domain and commercial implementations of the roughly 100 protocols of TCP/IP protocol suite became available in the 1980s. During the early 1990s, OSI protocol implementations also became available, and by the end of 1991 the Internet had grown to include some 5,000 networks in over three dozen countries, serving over 700,000 host computers used by over 4 million people. During the late 1980s, however, the population of Internet users and network constituents expanded internationally and began to include commercial facilities. Indeed, the bulk of the system today is made up of private networking facilities in educational and research institutions, businesses, and in government organizations across the globe. The Coordinating Committee for Intercontinental Networks (CCIRN), which was organized by the U.S. Federal Networking Council (FNC) and the European Reseaux Associees pour la Recherche Europeenne (RARE), plays an important role in the coordination of plans for government-sponsored research networking. CCIRN efforts have been a stimulus for the support of international cooperation in the Internet environment.

Today, as it was conceived in the late 1950s, the Internet remains a decentralized, open architecture system without a central hub [3]. Any computer on the system may connect to any other computer by way of a protocol TCP/IP standard. The operation of the Internet is not managed or controlled by any one body, although there are several bodies responsible for the technical aspects of its operation. The first of these is the Internet Architecture Board, comprised of the Internet Engineering Task Force and the Internet Research Task Force, which together are home to an international community of network designers, vendors, and researchers concerned with Internet architecture. Another body is the World Wide Web Consortium, an Internet industry consortium devoted to developing common protocols. An additional and important body worth mentioning is the Internet Corporation for Assigned Names and Numbers (ICANN), a nonprofit corporation founded to assign and manage domain names. These organizations operate informally and independent of one another, though they occasionally collaborate on aspects of their work. Finally, on the most basic level, are the various Internet service providers (ISPs), corporations that provide access to the Internet, to individuals, and to other corporations pursuant to terms of agreement entered into by the parties. ISPs also provide and regulate their users' access to e-mail, Web site hosting, newsgroups and bulletin boards, and similar services. The intricacies of how users access the Internet and the means by which they communicate are detailed in the Appendix.

The role of the Internet in business

A 1997 report issued by the U.S. government, entitled *A Framework for Global Electronic Commerce* [4], described how the Internet had transformed almost every aspect of everyday life. Regarding the Internet's effect on business and commerce, the report stated:

> As the Internet empowers citizens and democratizes societies, it is also changing classic business and economic paradigms. New models of commercial interaction are developing as businesses and consumers participate in the electronic marketplace and reap the resultant benefits.

> Entrepreneurs are able to start new businesses more easily, with smaller up-front investment requirements, by accessing the Internet's worldwide network of customers. Internet technology is having a profound effect on the global trade in services. World trade involving computer software, entertainment products (motion pictures, videos, games, sound recordings), information services (databases, on-line newspapers), technical information, product licenses, financial services, and professional services (businesses and technical consulting, accounting, architectural design, legal advice, travel services, etc.) has grown rapidly in the past decade, now accounting for well over $40 billion of U.S. exports alone.

An increasing share of these transactions occurs on-line. The GII has the potential to revolutionize commerce in these and other areas by dramatically lowering transaction costs and facilitating new types of commercial transactions. The Internet will also revolutionize retail and direct marketing. Consumers will be able to shop in their homes for a wide variety of products from manufacturers and retailers all over the world. They will be able to view these products on their computers or televisions, access information about the products, visualize the way the products may fit together (constructing a room of furniture on their screen, for example), and order and pay for their choice, all from their living rooms.

Initially, some businesses and many consumers were wary of transacting on the Internet due to the unknown and unique nature of the medium, as well as the lack of a settled set of legal rules that applied to on-line transactions. Many voiced concerns about enforcement of contracts and intellectual property rights, security and privacy, and the potential ability and reach of courts and governments to regulate what happens in cyberspace. Nonetheless, this initial hesitation soon gave way to open a new frontier of commercial possibilities, and on-line commerce was at least partly accountable for the tremendous economic growth seen in the 1990s [5]. Today, the Internet is, and will remain for the long term, both a forum of and a tool for facilitating commercial activity [6].

The legal environment of the Internet

The rapid spread of the Internet as a tool of commerce and communication has far outpaced the law and the legal system. Ordinarily, the law is a deliberative and gradualist entity that evolves to meet the needs of society. With the Internet, the law has had to quickly adapt to serve this function. Although this is a book about Internet law, it may come as some surprise to learn there is at this time no formalized, settled body of law that exclusively regulates the Internet. Rather, the law that governs the Internet—and that we will explore in the remainder of this book—is drawn from a variety of sources. There are several statutes that have been enacted by the state and federal governments that specifically address legal rights and liabilities that arise in cyberspace. More common, however, are the myriad of court opinions in which judges have applied existing legal principles and doctrines developed in the pre-Internet world to the various controversies and issues that have arisen in cyberspace. Thus, the legislatures and the courts have responded to Internet-based legal disputes by drawing from past precedents and applying them in a new setting or, in some areas, by enacting legislation that addresses a narrow set of problems that did not before exist.

The topics discussed in the chapters that follow present the opportunities as well as the legal risks posed by doing business on the Internet. With a working understanding of these risks, they can be managed in such a way as to maximize the potential offered by the Internet as a medium of communication and commerce.

Endnotes

[1] For historical treatments of the development of computers, see Ceruzzi, P. E., *A History of Modern Computing*, Cambridge, MA: MIT Press, 1998; Campbell-Kelly, M., and W. Aspray, *Computer: A History of the Information Machine*, New York: BasicBooks, 1996.

[2] Rawlins, G. J. E., *Moths to the Flame: The Seductions of Computer Technology,* MIT Press, 1996, pp. 72–74, archives.obs-us.com/obs/english/books/rawlins/moths/connect/1.html.

[3] Several authors have created graphical representations of the "topology" of cyberspace and its interconnectivity. See www.cybergeography.org/atlas/topology.html. To contrast the Internet in 1969, when it was known as ARPANET, and the now amazingly complex and interdependent economic structure of the Internet today, compare http://som.csudh.edu/cis/lpress/history/arpamaps/press.jpg with http://www.orgnet.com/netindustry.html.

[4] Clinton, W. J., and A. Gore, Jr., *A Framework for Global Electronic Commerce*, 1997, http://www.ecommerce.gov/framewrk.htm.

[5] For an in-depth summary of these changes, see U.S. Dept. of Commerce, *Digital Economy 2000*, June 2000, http://www.esa.doc.gov/de2k.htm.

[6] For more on the historical and socioeconomic growth of the Internet, see Leiner, B. A., et al., *A Brief History of the Internet,* 2000, www.isoc.org/internet/history/brief.html; Rowland, D., "Cyberspace—A Contemporary Utopia?" *J. Info., L. & Tech* (JILT), Vol. 3, 1998, www.law.warwick.ac.uk/jilt/98-3/rowland.html; Anderson, C., "The Accidental Superhighway," *The Economist,* Vol. 353, July 1, 1995, www.temple.edu/ lawschool/dpost/accidentalsuperhighway.htm.

2

The reach of legal jurisdiction over the Internet

The law relating to contract formation, tort liability, property, and other civil law issues of business transactions may differ in important ways from state to state and nation to nation. The threshold question in resolving these issues may turn on which court can exercise its jurisdiction over the parties in a civil legal dispute. Jurisdiction is the ability of a court to exercise its authority over the parties involved in the dispute and to issue a judgment that is binding on the parties. Unless a court has jurisdiction over the dispute, any judgment that it renders will be unenforceable.

Traditionally, the reach of a court's civil jurisdiction is grounded in geography and territorial borders. Because the Internet spans geographic and territorial borders, however, those who communicate or transact business there may be subject to the laws and jurisdiction of various and sometimes distant real-world forums. The Internet allows businesses to engage in business all over the world. In fact, a business' ability to reach such a broad audience on the Internet has presented unique questions about which courts can resolve disputes resulting from a business' contacts with citizens in its forum.

This chapter will describe how conflicts may arise regarding which forum's law may apply, where disputes may be resolved, and how to limit the possibility that one might be forced to litigate a dispute in a distant jurisdiction. Although the law of jurisdiction as applied to the Internet is currently evolving, this chapter will describe the main themes and guideposts that the courts have so far defined in resolving the reach of legal jurisdiction over the Internet.

The nature and scope of legal jurisdiction

Within the United States, there are two parallel court systems: a federal system and a system for each of the states, territories, and the District of Columbia. In order to exercise its authority over the parties involved in a civil dispute and to issue a judgment that is binding on those parties, a federal court must have *subject matter jurisdiction* and a state court must have both *subject matter* and either *personal* or *in rem jurisdiction*. Jurisdictional issues are often highly complex matters of court procedure and involve careful weighing of the facts of the case. This section will provide an overview of the essential aspects of jurisdiction. We begin by examining the subject matter jurisdiction of the federal courts, and then turn to the often more complicated issue of state court jurisdiction.

Federal court jurisdiction

In the federal court system, a court has two bases for exercising its authority over the type of dispute involved in the case, otherwise known as its subject matter jurisdiction: federal question jurisdiction and diversity jurisdiction. The federal court's subject matter jurisdiction typically extends only to those defendants who would also fall under the in rem or personal jurisdiction of the state where the federal court is located. This aspect of jurisdiction is discussed later.

Federal question jurisdiction exists when the case "arises under" or involves a claim under the United States Constitution, a treaty with a foreign nation, or a federal law [1]. For instance, a federal court could hear cases involving an issue of freedom of speech under the First Amendment to the Constitution, or a violation of the Civil Rights Act of 1964, or a claim of patent infringement. All of these are types of cases or subject matter that falls within the purview of a federal court. Alternatively, if the case does not involve a federal claim, the plaintiff may be able to bring suit in federal court under diversity jurisdiction.

A federal court may apply its diversity jurisdiction when two requirements are met. First, the amount of money damages in dispute must exceed $75,000 [2]. Second, the dispute must be between citizens of different states. As to the first requirement, the amount in controversy is measured not by what the plaintiff will actually recover if the plaintiff wins the case, but by the amount of damages that the plaintiff is reasonably entitled to request. None of the plaintiffs may be a resident of the same home states of any of the defendants. For example, there would be no diversity jurisdiction where plaintiffs from Nevada and California sued defendants from Arizona and Nevada. For purposes of diversity jurisdiction, a corporation is a citizen of both the state where it has been incorporated as well as the state in which it has its principal place of business.

In addition, both requirements must be met; otherwise, the court cannot exercise diversity jurisdiction over the case. If both requirements cannot be met, then the federal court can decide the case using federal question jurisdiction if the requirement of a federal claim of the type discussed above is involved. If neither the requirements for diversity jurisdiction nor federal question jurisdiction are present, the federal court lacks authority to hear the case and the parties must bring the suit in a state court that has jurisdiction.

State court jurisdiction

In order to adjudicate the case, a state court must have both subject matter and either personal or in rem jurisdiction over the dispute. As with the federal courts, the case must be of the type that the particular state court is entitled to exercise its authority. Some state courts are specialized as to their subject matter jurisdiction and may not hear cases outside of that area. For instance, the Court of Chancery in Delaware is a specialized court that may decide issues of corporate and business law, but that has no jurisdiction over matters of family law or probate law. Likewise, a criminal court cannot decide civil disputes such as breach of contract or negligence.

Even if the state court has subject matter jurisdiction, it also must have either in rem or personal jurisdiction. In rem jurisdiction is based on the location or presence of property within the borders of the state. If a defendant has property within the state, then the state has the authority to decide a dispute involving rights to or in that property, even though the defendant resides in another state. For instance, a Pennsylvania state court can decide a controversy about title to land located in Pennsylvania, or ownership of a boat docked on a Pennsylvania river, even if the land or boat is owned by a defendant who resides in Ohio.

By contrast, personal jurisdiction is based on the location or activities of a defendant within the borders of the state. Thus, an out-of-state defendant who agrees by contract to litigate a case within the state is subject to the state's personal jurisdiction. Similarly, a nonresident defendant might consent to personal jurisdiction by coming to the state to defend a suit brought there. What is more likely, however, is that the defendant will be unwillingly subject to the state court's jurisdiction by way of a long arm statute.

A long arm statute is a law enacted by the state's legislature that will subject an out-of-state defendant to the state court's jurisdiction when certain requirements are met. If these requirements are met, then the "long arm of the law" can reach over the state's borders and pull the defendant into court for purposes of litigating the suit. Long arm statutes usually specify the types of activities that would subject a defendant to jurisdiction. By way of example, here is an excerpt from the Missouri long arm statute:

> Any person or firm, whether or not a citizen or resident of this state, or any corporation, who in person or through an agent, does any of the acts enumerated in this section, thereby submits such person, firm, or corporation, and, if an individual, his personal representative, to the jurisdiction of the courts of this state as to any cause of action arising from the doing of an of such acts:
>
> (1) The transaction of any business within this state ...
>
> (3) The commission of a tortious act within this state .... [3]

Thus, under the Missouri statute, which is typical of all long arm statutes, a nonresident defendant may be subject to the state court's jurisdiction if the defendant does business in the state by entering into contracts with its residents. Alternatively, a nonresident defendant that engages in conduct that amounts to a tort, perhaps by driving carelessly or selling defective products that cause injury to a resident of the state, may be sued there as well.

If a defendant falls within the scope of one the categories enumerated in the long arm statute, the state court must also make sure that the defendant has sufficient *minimum contacts* with the state before it can exercise its jurisdiction over the defendant. In the words of the United States Supreme Court, the state court must decide, on the basis of the particular facts of the case and the nature of the defendant's connections with the state, whether extending its jurisdiction would not offend "traditional notions of fair play and substantial justice" [4]. This has proved to be a very difficult concept to define with any degree of specificity. Indeed, there are many factors that courts may consider in making this determination, including: whether, based on the level of defendant's conduct and contacts with the state, it was foreseeable that he or she would be required to litigate in the state's courts; whether the defendant has intentionally directed his or her activities to the residents of the state; whether the defendant has purposefully entered into the economic market of the state or taken advantage of the other benefits of doing business in the state; and whether the defendant's contacts with the state were continuous or substantial.

As can be seen, there is no definitive rule that easily answers the question of whether a state court has jurisdiction over the person of the defendant. Perhaps the best that can be said about this standard is that the greater the number of intended contacts and the longer these contacts continue, the greater the likelihood that the state court will be able to exercise its jurisdiction over the defendant. On the other hand, if the contacts are limited, insubstantial, or incidental, it is less likely that the defendant will be subject to personal jurisdiction. The courts will carefully scrutinize the facts of the case before requiring an out-of-state defendant to litigate in its forum. Furthermore, the analysis outlined above is approximately the same as that applied when the question of jurisdiction is international.

Jurisdictional issues in cyberspace

As we have just seen, the reach of a court's civil jurisdiction is closely tied to notions of territorial borders and presence or activity within those borders. Cyberspace, however, is not bounded geographically in the traditional sense; rather, it transcends territorial borders with its ability to simultaneously reach people all over the country and the world. Assuming that it has proper subject matter jurisdiction, how will a court in the real world determine whether it has personal jurisdiction of a nonresident defendant that may have engaged in a commercial transaction with someone in the forum state that did not also involve any physical contacts? So far, the answer to this question is that the court will apply the same framework described above in the context of the facts involving an Internet-based commercial transaction with a citizen of the forum state.

Initial attempts to define jurisdiction

The first several courts to confront the issue of jurisdiction based on on-line commercial activities applied the legal standards outlined above to reach sometimes inconsistent conclusions. Many of the cases involved disputes about on-line contractual transactions or trademarks, and the extent of the nonresident defendant's contacts was common factor in the court's analysis in each instance. Three examples illustrate how the courts have addressed the issue.

In the case of *CompuServe, Inc. v. Patterson* [5], Patterson, a Texas defendant, had subscribed to CompuServe's Internet service and had entered into two on-line contracts with CompuServe to write software for distribution as shareware on CompuServe's service. The contracts contained provisions that stated that they were entered into in Ohio and governed by Ohio law. The defendant electronically transmitted several files to CompuServe in Ohio, where they were stored and made available for sale and downloading to CompuServe subscribers. After a dispute as to whether CompuServe had infringed Patterson's trademark, an Ohio federal appellate court held that the Texas defendant was subject to jurisdiction in Ohio. The court based its decision on the fact that the defendant had a sufficient number of contacts with Ohio. He had entered into contracts that expressly stated that they were made in Ohio and governed by Ohio law, had sent files to Ohio for storage on CompuServe's system, and used that system to advertise and distribute his software to CompuServe's other subscribers.

Likewise, a Connecticut federal court in *Inset Systems, Inc. v. Instruction Set, Inc.* [6] held that a Connecticut business could sue a Massachusetts company for trademark infringement based on its use of the domain name Inset.com. The court's decision found that because Connecticut residents could easily access the Massachusetts company's Web site, on which appeared a toll-free telephone number that the court viewed as advertising, the company had purposefully availed itself of the opportunity to do business in Connecticut.

Conversely, in *Bensusan Restaurant Corp. v. King* [7], a federal court in New York found that it did not have jurisdiction over the a case involving a claim of trademark infringement brought by the owner of a New York jazz club called The Blue Note against a defendant in Missouri who also operated a night club called The Blue Note. The Missouri defendant had created a Web site that advertised his business but did not sell tickets to anyone in New York or anywhere else using the Internet. The court declined to exercise personal jurisdiction over the Missouri defendant because he had done nothing to target or encourage customers from New York to access his site, nor did he conduct any other business activities there.

The *Zippo* case and the sliding scale of jurisdiction

In 1997, a federal district court located in western Pennsylvania decided the issue of jurisdiction in the case of *Zippo Manufacturing Co. v. Zippo Dot Com, Inc.* [8]. The case involved a trademark infringement dispute over an Internet domain name. Zippo Manufacturing Company (ZMC) was a Pennsylvania corporation that manufactured tobacco lighters under the "Zippo" registered trademark. Zippo Dot Com (ZDC), a California corporation that operated a Web site and on-line news service, had registered "zippo.com," "zippo.net," and "zipponews.com" as domain names. ZMC objected, arguing that ZDC's use of the word "zippo" in its domain names was confusingly similar to and diminished the value of its trademark, and sued ZDC in federal court. ZDC attempted to dismiss the suit by contending that the court lacked personal jurisdiction to hear the case.

ZDC's Web site contained information about the company, advertisements, and an application for its Internet news service. A customer who wished to subscribe to the news service filled out an on-line application that asked for a variety of information, including the person's name and address. Payment was made by credit card over the Internet or the telephone. The application was then processed and the subscriber was assigned a password, which permitted the subscriber to view and download newsgroup messages stored on the ZDC's server in California.

ZDC's contacts with Pennsylvania occurred almost exclusively over the Internet. Its offices, employees, and Internet servers were located in California, and it maintained no offices, employees, or agents in Pennsylvania. ZDC's advertising for its service to Pennsylvania residents involved posting information about its service on its Web site. At the time it was sued, ZDC had approximately 140,000 paying subscribers worldwide. Approximately 2%, or 3,000, of those subscribers were Pennsylvania residents. Additionally, ZDC had entered into agreements with seven Internet access providers in Pennsylvania to permit their subscribers to access its news service, and two of those providers were located in western Pennsylvania.

In analyzing the issue of personal jurisdiction, the court first decided that ZDC was covered by the part of the Pennsylvania long arm statute authorizing the exercise of jurisdiction over nonresident defendants that contract to supply services or things in Pennsylvania. The court found that ZDC had done this by contracting to supply Internet news services to approximately 3,000 Pennsylvania residents and entering into agreements with seven Internet access providers in Pennsylvania. Next, the court reviewed some of the cases discussed above and then observed that their outcomes suggested a sliding scale for determining whether jurisdiction exists:

> [T]he likelihood that personal jurisdiction can be constitutionally exercised is directly proportionate to the nature and quality of commercial activity that an entity conducts over the Internet. This sliding scale is consistent with well developed personal jurisdiction principles. At one end of the spectrum are situations where a defendant clearly does business over the Internet. If the defendant enters into contracts with residents of a foreign jurisdiction that involve the knowing and repeated transmission of computer files over the Internet, personal jurisdiction if proper. At the opposite end are situations where a defendant has simply posted information on an Internet Web site which is accessible to users in foreign jurisdictions. A passive Web site that does little more than make information available to those who are interested in it is not grounds for the exercise personal jurisdiction. The middle ground is occupied by interactive Web sites where a user can exchange information with the host computer. In these cases, the exercise of jurisdiction is determined by examining the level of interactivity and commercial nature of the exchange of information that occurs on the Web site [9].

Applying this standard to the facts of the *Zippo* case, the court concluded that ZDC fell into the middle category and that it had jurisdiction over ZDC because it actively solicited business in Pennsylvania and knowingly contracted with numerous Pennsylvania residents. In addition, the court pointed out that the alleged trademark infringement occurred in Pennsylvania and that it had a strong interest in resolving trademark disputes involving Pennsylvania businesses such as ZMC. As such, the court determined that it could appropriately exercise personal jurisdiction over ZDC [10].

The international dimension of Internet jurisdiction

By its very nature, doing business on the Internet involves an international aspect. As the expanse of electronic commerce continues to widen, courts will be called upon to resolve disputes that span national borders. Thus, any business engaged in on-line commercial transactions must consider seriously the risks of being sued and forced to defend the suit in a foreign country. To date, there have been few reported cases to provide clear guidance in this area, and there is no international court or rule of procedure that clearly defines when a business based in one country will be subject to the jurisdiction of another country's court system. However, it is instructive to review a few general principles of international law and procedure.

Generally speaking, the courts of one country have jurisdiction to adjudicate a dispute or enforce a judgment if the laws of the forum country can reasonably be applied to the persons and circumstances involved in the dispute. Whether it is reasonable for a court to exercise jurisdiction depends on whether the foreign defendant was doing business within the country, engaging in activities likely to have substantial, direct, and foreseeable effect within the country [11]. The facts and circumstances of the transaction giving rise to the dispute, rather than the defendant's nationality, are key.

In *Braintech, Inc. v. Kostiuk* [12], a Canadian appellate court in British Columbia refused to enforce judgment entered by a Texas court, on the grounds that Texas had no jurisdiction in an action brought by Canadian company against a Vancouver resident for allegedly defamatory comments made in an on-line chat forum. Although the Canadian company had an office in Texas, the court held that the defendant would have to establish some link to forum state, such as residency or doing business, to be subject to jurisdiction.

By contrast, a British court in *Mecklermedia Corp. v. D.C. Congress GmbH* [13] concluded that it had jurisdiction to resolve a suit brought by a U.S. company for the tort of "passing off" against a German company. The suit arose from the alleged infringement of the U.S. company's trademark "Internet World," on a German defendant's Web site. The British court held that jurisdiction was proper in the United Kingdom, notwithstanding the fact that the defendant's Web site was hosted in Germany, because it was the goodwill of the plaintiff's trademark in the United Kingdom that was alleged to have been damaged.

There is a strong similarity between the principles discussed in these cases and the standards that apply in the United States as explained earlier. Thus, the *Zippo* sliding scale of fact-specific factors relating to interactivity might function as a rough guideline as well [14]. Indeed, the Canadian court in *Braintech* cited and discussed the *Zippo* case in reaching its decision. In addition, a proposed treaty known as the Hague Convention on Jurisdiction and Foreign Judgments in Civil and Commercial Matters [15] may dramatically expand the scope of international jurisdiction. The Hague Convention is intended to assure that judgments issued by a court in one country are enforced by other countries and to establish jurisdictional rules governing transnational disputes. The Convention, if widely adopted, will allow the courts of its member nations to more easily determine when they can and cannot adjudicate such cases [16].

Limiting the reach of jurisdiction by a court in a distant forum

This chapter has explained how federal and state courts determine when they can subject a business to suit. The standards for determining subject matter and in rem jurisdiction [17] are often fairly straightforward, but the standards applied for determining personal jurisdiction are inexact even under the *Zippo* test. The sliding scale has been adopted and applied by a number of other courts since the case was decided in 1997 [18]. It has proved to be a useful guideline in defining the scope of jurisdiction, but from the standpoint of practical planning, it is impossible to predict with certainty when or where a business engaged in electronic commerce may be sued. Nevertheless, there are several steps that a business can take to limit the risk of being forced to defend a lawsuit in a distant forum.

Perhaps the easiest and most obvious way to avoid being subject to the jurisdiction of a particular forum is to avoid doing any business in that forum or with its residents. If there are no contacts with a particular state, there will be no jurisdiction. By way of illustration, a business should state clearly on its Web site that it will not accept offers from or transact business with residents of a particular state and, if an on-line application or order form is used, block access by those customers from that state. Another means of addressing the problem is to follow the *Zippo* sliding scale standard and post a passive, noninteractive Web site. Such a Web site functions merely as an on-line advertisement or informational notice, which is accessible but not targeted to users in foreign jurisdictions.

If it is impractical to use a passive Web site because it will severely decrease business, then it may be necessary to use a more interactive site, where a user can exchange information with the host computer. Under *Zippo*, such a Web site will fall within the middle ground of the sliding scale and the exercise of jurisdiction will be determined by examining the level of interactivity and commercial nature of the exchange of information that occurs on the site. In such instances, it would be important to limit all other real-world contacts with and promotional activities directed to the foreign jurisdiction.

Should these solutions be undesirable or impractical, then another option is to incorporate forum selection and choice of law clauses in the on-line agreement with a customer. A forum selection clause is a contract provision by which the parties agree that any disputes will be resolved in a certain court or state, while a choice of law clause specifies which state's law will be applied in resolving the dispute. For instance, a business based in New York might provide language in the on-line contract that any disputes will be litigated in a court located in New York and that the law of Delaware (because its contract law may more favorable to sellers) will be applied in interpreting the contract. A potential problem, however, is that many courts require that such provisions be reasonable in order to be enforceable. At the very least, a business should make certain that these provisions are conspicuous and understandable to the buyer.

A more drastic protective measure would be to spin off the Internet-based division of the business and incorporate and operate it separate from the rest of the business. Maintaining the on-line part of the business as a separate legal entity may shield the assets of the principal part of the business from liability in the event of an adverse judgment. Doing this, however, does not remove the threat of being required to litigate in a distant forum, but it may provide a degree of protection to the non-on-line aspects of the enterprise.

Endnotes

[1] 28 U.S.C. § 1331.

[2] *Id.* § 1332.

[3] Mo. Rev. Stat. § 506.500. The Missouri statute was discussed in the case of *Maritz, Inc. v. Cybergold, Inc.*, 947 F. Supp. 1328 (E.D. Mo. 1996), where the court held that a Web site owner in California, which solicited Missouri subscribers for its e-mail mailing list service, was subject to Missouri court jurisdiction.

[4] *World-Wide Volkswagen Corp. v. Woodson*, 444 U.S. 286, 297, 1980.

[5] 89 F.3d 1257 (6th Cir. 1996).

[6] 937 F. Supp. 161 (D. Conn. 1996).

[7] 937 F. Supp. 295 (S.D.N.Y. 1996).

[8] 952 F. Supp. 1119 (W.D. Pa. 1997).

[9] 952 F. Supp. at 1124.

[10] The courts since *Zippo* have considered a variety of facts in determining whether jurisdiction was proper. See, for example, *Dostana Enters LLC v. Federal Express Corp.*, No. 0747(RWS) (S.D.N.Y. 2000) (location of Web site server not relevant to determining jurisdiction); *Winfield Collection Ltd. v. McCauley*, No. 99-CV-75875-DT (E.D. Mich. 2000) (sale of items on eBay auction site did not establish minimum contacts for jursidiction); *Morantz v. Hang & Shine Ultrasonics, Inc.*, 1999 U.S. Dist LEXIS 19412 (E.D. Pa. 1999) (Web site with toll-free phone number did not expose defendant to jurisdiction); *Hurley v. Cancun Playa Oasis Int'l Hotels*, No. 99-574 (E.D. Pa. 1999) (same); *3DO Co. v. Poptop Software, Inc.*, 1998 U.S. Dist. LEXIS 21281 (N.D. Cal. 1998) (jurisdiction proper because Web site was interactive and conduct had effect in forum state); *Digital Equip. Corp. v. Altavista Tech., Inc.*, 960 F. Supp. 456 (D. Mass. 1997) (defendant's Web site and breach of contract in forum establish jurisdiction).

[11] *See* Restatement (Third) of the Foreign Relations Law of the United States §§ 403 & 421.

[12] BCCA 0169 (B.C. Ct. App. 1999).

[13] High Court TLR (March 27, 1997).

[14] The American Bar Association's Jurisdiction in Cyberspace Project has issued an extensive report concerning transnational jurisdiction and the Internet. See American Bar Association, *Achieving Legal and Business Order in Cyberspace: A Report on Global Jurisdiction Issues Created by the Internet*, 2000, www.abanet.org/buslaw/cyber/initiatives/jurisdiction.html.

[15] For the text of this proposed treaty and related materials, see www.hcch.net.

[16] See Sandburg, B., "Vague Hague Treaty Causes a Stir," *The Recorder*, Feb. 8, 2001 (discussing e-business opposition to the treaty).

[17] In rem jurisdiction, which is based on the property that is the subject of the dispute, remains an alternative basis on which a plaintiff may bring suit. In the case of *Porsche Cars North America, Inc. v. Prosch.com*, F. Supp. (E.D. Va. 1999), the plaintiff argued that a domain name could be the type of property that formed the source of in rem jurisdiction. The federal court, however, rejected this argument.

[18] A federal appellate court in Texas applied the *Zippo* sliding scale test in the case of *Mink v. AAAA Development*, F.3d (5th Cir. 1999). The court held: "While [the Vermont defendant's] website provides users with a printable mail-in order form, AAAA's toll-free number, a mailing address and an electronic (e-mail) address, orders are not taken through AAAA's website. This does not classify the website as anything more than passive advertisement."

3

Using encryption and authentication in electronic communication

Electronic data encoding, or encryption, is an important tool in electronic contracts and communications. Encryption ensures the confidentiality of electronic communications and data against the risk of theft, misuse, or alteration. Many businesses now use robust encryption technologies to secure such information while in storage or in transmission in order to prevent theft of trade secrets [1] and interception of commercial data and communications. Similarly, many individuals use encryption in their private communications to ensure their privacy and to prevent identity fraud. At the same time, encryption technology must be used in such a way as to avoid violating federal espionage and export laws.

In addition, closely related tools known as electronic authentication and digital signatures play an increasingly important role in electronic commercial transactions. Authentication technology ensures the integrity and authenticity of the data transmitted. In other words, authentication ensures trust in the agreement formation process. As business moves inexorably into cyberspace, the need for attribution devices to authenticate the identities of merchants and sellers will continue to grow. Indeed, federal and state legislators have begun to underscore this inevitable reality by enacting measures that not only approve of, but also promote the use of electronic authentication.

This chapter considers the use and legal aspects of using digital encryption and authentication technologies in the on-line marketplace. Encryption is considered in the context of the regulatory scheme that controls its use and export. Next, the role and use of digital authentication is discussed as an emerging facilitator of electronic commercial transactions.

What is digital encryption?

The idea behind digital encryption is quite simple: using a computer program, a mathematical equation, known as an encryption algorithm, encodes and converts a plaintext message using a key into unintelligible ciphertext. Consider, for example, where the plaintext message "HELLO" is encrypted into cyphertext using a key that shifts the letters of each word by one to the following letter in the alphabet: HELLO IFMMP [2]. The length of a key is measured in bits—the digits 0 and 1 used to encode the data. The greater the number of bits, the more secure the key is considered. In addition, the level of difficulty a third party would have in breaking the code determines the strength of a key and the robustness of the encryption algorithm. Thus, the longer the mathematical algorithm is employed, the more secure is the encryption system.

There are two basic types of encryption methods that are commonly available. In a private key encryption system, sometimes referred to as secret key or symmetric key systems, the key used to encode the information is sent to the recipient, who then uses it to decode the encrypted message. The principal concern with using private key encryption is the risk involved in sending the key to the intended recipient. Key management is essential; the sender and recipient must use a separate and secure channel, or protocol, to agree on and transfer a common key. Prudent key management requires that keys be retired and replaced at periodic intervals to prevent intruders from using exemplars of ciphertext to break the key. As such, the level of security in a public key encryption system is directly related to the security of the key's delivery.

On the other hand, in a public key encryption system, also referred to as dual key or asymmetric key systems, there are two mathematically related keys: a private key and a public key. Using a private key, a user can encode a message that can only be decrypted with his or her public key. In similar fashion, the user can use the recipient's public key to encrypt a message, which can only be decoded with the recipient's private key and no other. The risk of key security is thereby reduced. Nonetheless, key management remains important, in that the message sender's private key must remain confidential to avoid unauthorized use. Additionally, ensuring that the public key really belongs to the sender requires the involvement of a certification authority—a reliable third party that attributes a public key with a specific individual.

Aside from these two most commonly used encryption systems, there are other methods for securely transmitting data. One such method is steganography, sometimes referred to as watermarking or fingerprinting, whereby one message is hidden within another. A digital steganographic system embeds or encodes one piece of information within the unused areas of video or audio files. Steganography replaces these unused portions of the file with indelible information that can be covertly transmitted with the file [3]. Another type of secure transmission system is known as chaffing and winnowing, by which it is possible to hide a message by breaking it into packets that are then secretly identified as good information, or wheat, and bogus information, or chaff, in such a way that an interceptor cannot distinguish between them unless he or she has the authentication key [4].

Regulation of digital encryption technology

Digital encryption is treated as a dual use technology. A dual use technology is one that has both military and civilian uses. The increasing use of encryption has led to concerns by federal law enforcement and national security authorities that these technologies will be used for criminal and terrorist purposes [5]. These concerns stem from the belief that the United States is vulnerable to electronic attack and on-line crime. Some of the fears expressed by law enforcement personnel are that digital cryptography could be used for drug trafficking, terrorism, espionage, and theft. As a consequence, the present United States encryption regulatory regime is an outgrowth of these concerns, and the government has sought to control the development and diffusion of digital encryption technologies through the use of export controls.

There are no restrictions on the manufacture, import, sale, or use of encryption technologies within the United States. The export of encryption, however, is governed by the Arms Export Control Act (AECA) [6], which is administered by the State Department under the International Traffic in Arms Regulations (ITAR) [7], and the Export Administration Act (EAA) [8], along with the Export Administration Regulations (EAR) [9], which are administered by the Commerce Department. For a while, most encryption software was also categorized as a munition and its export was restricted by the State Department. In December 1996, however, control over the export of encryption products was turned over to the Commerce Department, where they are currently regulated as encryption items [10].

In general, one needs a license in order to export encryption items, which include all encryption commodities, software, and technology that contain encryption features and are subject to the EAR. The export of encryption source code is defined as "downloading, or causing the downloading of, such software to locations...outside of the United States..." [11]. Some types of encryption items are exempted, including access control equipment (such as automatic teller machines, self-service statement printers, or point-of-sale terminals) that protects password or personal identification numbers to prevent unauthorized access; and cryptographic equipment specially designed and limited for use in banking or money transactions [12]. Also exempted is data authentication equipment that calculates a message authentication code (MAC) or similar result to ensure no alteration of text has taken place or to authenticate users [13].

Federal efforts to regulate encryption have not been limited to restrictions on exports. In 1995, the government launched the Clipper Chip initiative in an attempt to establish an encryption standard accessible to law enforcement authorities only by court order. The government explained that the purpose of the initiative was to allow it to thwart terrorism, drug trafficking, foreign espionage, and other crimes that might make use of encryption technology to elude surveillance and detection. Pursuant to this program, all electronic encryption technology was to be subject to key escrow, by which the government would hold copies of all the keys used for encrypting and decrypting messages. Notwithstanding its purpose, the Clipper Chip initiative provoked such an outcry of protest on constitutional and economic grounds that it was soon abandoned.

In December 1998, the United States persuaded the 33 nations that have signed the Wassenaar Arrangement on Export Controls for Conventional Arms and Dual Use Goods and Technologies [14], to apply the same strict export controls on encryption software as they apply to weapons. The Wassenaar Arrangement is intended to prevent, through cooperation among the participants, the acquisition and proliferation of armaments and sensitive dual-use technologies for military end uses. Under the 1998 agreement, Wassenaar participants restrict exports of general encryption products using more than 56-bit keys, but allow firms making commercial software for the mass market, such as Internet browsers or electronic mail programs, to use up to 64-bit keys. The agreement imposes no restraints on encryption used to protect entertainment products, such as video transmissions on the Internet, from piracy.

In October 2000, in response to the European Union's liberalization of its encryption export rules, the U.S. Commerce Department allowed the export of encryption products of any strength to the nations of the European Union, as well as Australia, Japan, New Zealand, Norway, Switzerland, Poland, Hungary, and the Czech Republic. U.S. exporters may now sell encryption technology to businesses in those countries and to their governments. American firms must first submit a commodity classification request form with the U.S. government, but may then ship the products without waiting for a review and clearance. In January 2000, the United States also eased the export restrictions on the export of high-speed computers that can be used to develop encryption systems. However, reexport of these computers, as well as encryption technology, to certain rogue nations—such as Iraq, Iran, Cuba, Libya, and North Korea—remains prohibited.

Freedom of speech challenges to encryption export controls

The federal government's encryption export regulations have been subject to several court challenges on the grounds that the federal export controls on the publication of encryption software source code amounted to a unconstitutional restraint on free speech [15]. In *Bernstein v. United States Dep't. of State* [16], the defendant, Daniel Bernstein, a graduate student at the University of California at Berkeley, wrote an encryption program that he named Snuffle. Bernstein, who wanted to post Snuffle on the Internet for use by other students, had submitted a commodity jurisdiction request to the Department of State to determine whether the program was subject to government regulation. After the State Department disallowed him to distribute the program, Bernstein sued, claiming that his First Amendment right of free speech had been violated.

The federal district court held that the Snuffle program's source code was speech under the First Amendment and that the government's licensing scheme was an illegal prior restraint on speech. In reaching this conclusion, the court reasoned that source code was "language" in that it is "the expression of ideas, commands [and] objectives" and that even though Snuffle may have been "essentially functional, that does not remove it from the realm of speech " [17].

On appeal, the Ninth Circuit Court of Appeals held that the EAR regulations were an unconstitutional prior restraint on speech that violated the First Amendment insofar as they prohibited the export of designated encryption software without a license. The court's decision was founded on its determination that the source code used in such encryption software is expressive speech entitled to protection under the First Amendment. The court analogized source code to equations and graphs used by mathematicians, which are also means used to express ideas. Finding that the source code constituted protectable speech, the court determined that the EAR's requirement that the plaintiff obtain a license before being permitted to export source code was an impermissible prior restraint on speech. Though such restraints are permitted in limited circumstances, they must, among other things, be limited to a preset brief period of time and permit expeditious review by a court. Because the EAR regulatory scheme did not set a time limit by which the government had to either pass on an application for a license or determine any appeal from such a ruling, the court held that it lacked the necessary procedural safeguards and was unconstitutional.

A second, similar challenge to the federal export controls was presented in *Karn v. United States Dep't. of State* [18]. In 1996, Philip Karn filed a lawsuit challenging the State Department's denial of permission to export a diskette containing the source code for several encryption algorithms printed in a book entitled *Applied Cryptography* by Bruce Schneier [19]. The State Department approved the export of the book itself, but not the diskette containing identical information. Like Bernstein, Karn argued that the export regulations were an impermissible restraint on freedom of speech. Karn sought review in federal district court of the government's denial claiming that the AECA and the ITAR were unconstitutional under the First and Fifth Amendments.

Although it agreed that encryption source code was speech for First Amendment purposes, the court rejected Karn's claims and upheld the constitutionality of the AECA and ITAR. The court found that the regulations did not offend the First Amendment because they were content-neutral, within the government's constitutional power to control the export of defense articles, and narrowly tailored to further the significant government interest in preventing proliferation of encryption technologies. Furthermore, the court held that the regulations did not violate Karn's due process rights because they were rationally based; that is, it was not irrational for the State Department to control export of the diskette but not control the export of the book containing the same information, because the book contained no machine-readable media.

Karn appealed, but on December 30, 1996, just before oral arguments were to be heard, the president transferred the responsibility for export regulation of civilian encryption software from the State Department to the Commerce Department. The court of appeals remanded the case to the district court for review under the Commerce Department's new Export Administration Regulations. In January 2000, after the new export regulations went into effect, publicly available encryption source code like that involved in Karn's lawsuit became exportable and Karn allowed his case to be dismissed as moot.

Finally, in the case of *Junger v. Daly* [20], Peter Junger sought to post encryption software on his Web site as part of his on-line class at Case Western Reserve University School of Law. Junger requested a permanent injunction against the government from enforcing the encryption software and technology provisions of EAR against anyone who seeks to disclose or export encryption technology. The court granted summary judgment in favor of the government, holding that the export of encryption source code on the Internet was not protected by the First Amendment. Specifically, the court held that the EAR "are constitutional because encryption source code is inherently functional, because the Export Regulations are not directed at source code's expressive elements, and because the Export Regulations do not reach academic discussions of software, or software in print form" [21]. On review, the court of appeals disagreed and held that the source code was protected by the First Amendment, but noted that national security interests can outweigh free speech interests and allow for regulation of the speech in certain instances. The appellate court remanded the case to the district court in order to examine the new export regulations and determine if Junger's challenge was supportable [22].

Given the nature of the issue involved, these cases are unlikely to be the last word on whether encryption coding is protectable as free speech. Nevertheless, the trend toward liberalized export regulations may make a great deal of the matter moot. The more flexible regulatory scheme will allow U.S. developers and sellers of encryption technology to be more competitive abroad. As a practical matter, the use of encryption to guarantee security and confidentiality of data in the business setting is necessity. Businesses should retain computer security experts to assess their needs and periodically monitor or audit the security of their encryption systems. Businesses that export encryption technology should pay close attention to and comply with export regulations, especially because encryption is still regulated as a matter of national security and because the regulations have been revised so frequently in the recent past. We now turn to a discussion of digital authentication and its increasingly important role in electronic commerce.

Authentication and contract formation

Electronic commerce is made possible by the formation of contracts between mutually assenting parties who desire to do business. For many years, the common law of contracts that arose from precedents decided over time, governed the formation and performance of agreements. However, with respect to sales of goods, differences between the states as to the rules applied to such transactions often resulted in confusion and unpredictability as firms expanded their businesses beyond their home states. In an effort to bring some consistency to this area of law, an organization of legal scholars, judges, and lawyers known as the National Conference of Commissioners of Uniform State Laws (NCCUSL) drafted the Uniform Commercial Code (UCC), which presented a set of uniform rules to be applied in commercial transactions. Beginning in the 1950s, the state legislatures began to adopt the UCC with the result that businesses engaged in interstate commerce could act with greater certainty in their dealings.

The onset of electronic commercial transactions has brought new challenges, which NCCUSL has sought to address in the form of two new uniform law proposals. The Uniform Computer Information Transactions Act (UCITA) applies to the licensing of computer software and provides a set of terms governing such transactions that apply when the parties do not address a particular issue in negotiating their license agreement. The Uniform Electronic Transaction Act (UETA) applies to electronic agreements and signatures. UETA is designed to ensure the enforceability of electronic contracts, giving them the same effect as paper contracts. In short, UETA guarantees that, in any state where a particular contract must be in writing and signed, these requirements can be satisfied by an electronic record and electronic signature. Both UETA and UCITA are under consideration by many states, and these proposed laws almost certainly signal the shape of electronic commerce to come.

Aside from what UETA and UCITA may accomplish, as a general matter, in any commercial transaction, the authentication of identity and mutual assent is a fundamental requirement to contract formation. While encryption has a role in this process, authentication by digital signatures or certificates has emerged as the principal means of addressing this need. Public key encryption can be used to generate a digital signature, which can be used to authenticate the identity of a sender of a message as well as its contents. A digital signature functions as a seal of verification that the message has not been modified without the sender's authorization [23].

Initially, the states took the lead in enacting legislation that recognized the validity of digital signatures in order to spur the development of reliable electronic transactions. In fact, Utah was the first state to enact a digital signature law in 1995, and since then a majority of the states have passed a variety of digital signature laws that take varying approaches. The use of digital signatures has been given further impetus by the enactment of the Electronic Signatures in Global and National Commerce Act, known also as the E-Sign Law [24]. This federal law took effect in October 2000, giving digital signatures the same legal standing as their handwritten counterparts. The E-Sign Law, which ensures that transactions cannot be denied effect simply because they are executed electronically, works hand in hand with state laws require an agreement to be in a signed writing and recognize digital authentication as a means of doing this electronically.

Generally speaking, state digital signature statutes follow one of three paths. Some states, such as Utah, acknowledge the legal validity only of digital signatures verified by a certification authority—a trusted third party, such as a government agency. Other states, such as Florida, provide that any type of digital signature is valid in place of a handwritten signature. Still other states, such as California and Virginia, require some minimal evidence that the signature is unique to or under the exclusive control of the sender, or that the electronic information has not been altered either during transmission or after receipt. In addition, certain states permit only transactions with government agencies to be effectuated through the use of digital signatures, while others permit only certain kinds of commercial transactions to be validated [25].

Let us consider the process of creating a digital signature using encryption. Recall that in a public key encryption system, the user has two keys—a public key available to everyone and a private key used only by the user. Anyone can use the public key to send an encrypted message to the user, but only the user can decrypt the message using the private key. Using the private key and authentication software, the user could affix a digital signature on electronic data and documents. The digital signature serves as a seal or stamp that is unique to the user and that ensures detection if the original data or document is intercepted and changed by another person while in transmission.

To create a digital signature, a hash, which is a numerical value representing the entire text of the message (and sometimes referred to as a message digest), must first be created. This is done by running the contents of the message through a computer program, known as a hash function, which processes the text and results in a unique numerical value. This value (the hash) is unique to the message because any subsequent change in the message text will also change the hash. Next, a digital signature is produced when the user employs his or her private key to encrypt the hash. The encrypted hash is appended to the data or document, which is then sent to the recipient. The hash means, in effect, that the message has been signed.

When the recipient receives the message, he or she runs the message through the same hash function program applied by the user in order to produce a second, separate hash. The recipient then decrypts the sender's hash with the user's public key and compares it to the second hash. If the two hash values are identical, the recipient knows that the original data or document has not been intercepted and changed along the way. In other words, the message is verified as being authentic to the user who sent it [26]. For most on-line consumers, however, the entire process of digital authentication occurs instantaneously when they click "OK" or "I Accept" at the end of an electronic contract.

The enactment of the E-Sign Law and similar state laws guarantees that electronic authentication will be a critical step in the contract formation process. Businesses that contract on-line must be prepared to authenticate their identities, the identities of their contractual counterparts, and their mutual agreements. Encryption is part of the process because it can safeguard the confidentiality of the transaction, and because a digital signature is nothing more than the encrypted hash of the text that has been sent. Moreover, when a public key encryption system is used, a trusted third party, or certificate authority, must be used to verify that a public key actually belongs to a certain party. The certification process will use an electronic means of authentication. Whether selecting an authentication technology to create a digital signature, or selecting a certificate authority, a business should pay special attention to the means used to protect its identifying information and to secure the integrity and confidentiality of the information transmitted. The use of encryption is another means of doing this, and encryption technologies will continue to play an increasingly important role in securing on-line commercial transactions, authenticating the transmission of data, and ensuring the secrecy of communications and proprietary information such as trade secrets.

Endnotes

[1] Encryption and authentication technology is invaluable in protecting on-line trade secrets and proprietary data and know-how. The law of trade secrets is discussed more fully in Chapter 4.

[2] For an extended explanation of digital encryption technology, see Garfinkle, S., and G. Spafford, *Web Security and Commerce*, Sebastapol, CA: O'Reilly & Associates, 1991, pp. 187–208. Excellent on-line sources of information about cryptographic terminology, methods, and software are available at: "Cryptography A-2-Z," (visited Oct. 4, 2000) http://www.ssh.fi/tech/crypto/; Fahn, P., "Answers to Frequently Asked Questions About Today's Cryptography," (visited Oct. 18, 2000), http://www.rsa.com/rsalabs/newfaq/.

[3] Detailed information about steganography is available at StegoArchive.com/members.tripod.com/steganography/stego.html.

[4] This method was developed by Ronald Rivest, who along with Adi Shamir and Leonard Adleman, developed the widely used RSA encryption algorithm. For a description of this method, see. Rivest, R. L., "Chaffing and Winnowing: Confidentiality Without Encryption," (rev. April 24, 1998), theory.lcs.mit.edu/~rivest/chaffing.txt.

[5] See "Impact of Encryption on Law Enforcement and Public Safety: Hearings Before the Senate Comm. on Commerce, Science, and Transportation," 104th Cong., 1996 (statement of Louis J. Freeh, Dir., Federal Bureau of Investigation). These concerns are also summarized in Chapters 3 and 4 of *Codes, Keys and Conflicts: Issues in U.S. Crypto Policy, Report of a Special Panel of the ACM U.S. Public Policy Committee (USACM)*, June 1994 (visited Dec. 8, 1998), http://info.acm.org/REPORTS/ACM_CRYPTO_STUDY/_WEB/c_report. html.

[6] Arms Export Control Act of 1976, Pub. L. No. 94-329, title II, 212(a)(1), 90 Stat. 744 (1976) (codified at 22 U.S.C. § 2778 (1994) (repealing the Mutual Security Act, ch 937, 68 Stat. 832 (1954)).

[7] 22 C.F.R. § 120.

[8] 50 U.S.C. § 2401.

[9] 15 C.F.R. § 730.

[10] The policies of most other countries are more liberal than that of the United States. For a survey of the cryptography policies of over 200 nations and territories around the world, see Madsen, W., et al., "Cryptography and Liberty: An International Survey of Encryption Policy," *J. Marshall J. Computer & Info. L.*, Vol. 16, 1998, pp. 475.

[11] *Id* § 734.2(b)(9).

[12] *Id.* § 734.2.

[13] *Id.*

[14] The text of the agreement as well as related materials are available on-line at http://www.wassenaar.org/.

[15] For an extended analyses of the First Amendment protection of encryption issue, see Park, E. J., "Protecting the Core Values of the First Amendment in an Age of New Technologies: Scientific Expression vs. National Security," *Va. J.L. & Tech.* ,Vol. 2, 1997, p. 3; Samoriski, J. H., et al., "Encryption and the First Amendment," *Comm. L. & Pol'y*, Vol. 2, 1997, p. 81; Reiman, P. E., Comment, "Cryptography and the First Amendment: The Right to Be Unheard," *J. Marshall J. Computer & Info., L.*, Vol. 14, 1996, p. 325, Note, E. L., "The Philip Zimmermann Investigation: The Start of the Fall of Export Restrictions on Encryption Software under First Amendment Free Speech Issues," *Syracuse L. Rev.*, Vol. 48, 1998, p. 130.

[16] 922 F. Supp. 1426 (N.D. Cal.) (denying motion to dismiss), *partial summary judgment granted,* 945 F. Supp. 1279 (1996), *superseded,* 974 F. Supp. 1288 (1997).

[17] 922 F. Supp. at 1435.

[18] 925 F. Supp. 1 (D.D.C. 1996), *remanded,* 107 F.3d 923 (D.C. Cir. 1997).

[19] See Schneier, B., *Applied Cryptography, 2nd Edition,* New York: John Wiley & Sons, 1996.

[20] 8 F. Supp. 708 (N.D. Ohio 1998). Junger's Web site on free speech and the export of crypto is located at http://samsara.law.cwru.edu/comp_law/crypto_export/.

[21] *Id.* at 712.

[22] *Junger v. Daley,* 2000 Fed. App. 0117P (6th Cir. 2000).

[23] "Intellectual Property and the National Information Infrastructure," The Rep. of the Working Group on Intell. Prop. Rts., 1995, p. 188.

[24] 15 U.S.C. § 7001.

[25] A useful survey of state digital signature legislation is available from the Internet Law and Policy Forum. See "Update: Survey of State Electronic and Digital Signature Legislative Initiatives," www.iplf.org/digsig/update.htm. For a database of state laws, including legislative summaries and status information, links to the state legislatures, as well as full text of bills, resolutions, and amendments, see www.mbc.com/ecommerce/state.asp.

[26] For an analysis of various identity authentication systems and authority authentication, see Ford, M. D., "Identity Authentication and 'E-Commerce,'" *J. Info., L. & Tech.*, Vol. 3, 1998, http://www.law.warwick.ac.uk/jilt/98-3/ford.html.

4

Trade secrets in electronic commerce

In the information age, when the entire business of a commercial enterprise might be based on the commercial value of the proprietary information it possesses, trade secret law offers a source of protection for that investment. The law of trade secrets protects nonpublic business information against unauthorized use or disclosure by another who obtained it through a confidential relationship or improper means. Trade secret protection is of potentially infinite duration, and there are no formal registration or application procedures that the owner must follow in order to legally protect a trade secret [1]. In this chapter, we consider the scope of protection afforded by trade secret law, and then examine how trade secret issues have arisen in the electronic environment. Finally, we will consider a number of practical strategies for using trade secret law to safeguard proprietary information.

The nature and extent of trade secret protection

Any information that provides a commercial advantage to a business can be a trade secret, though the secret is protected only if its owner had maintained it in actual secrecy and disclosed it to another only under an agreement of confidentiality. Trade secrets are protected by state law, and all but a few of the states have adopted the Uniform Trade Secrets Act, which defines a trade secret as any

> information, including a formula, pattern, compilation, program, device, method, technique, or process that:
>
> (i) derives independent economic value, actual or potential, from not being generally known to, and not being readily ascertainable by proper means by, other persons who can obtain economic value from its disclosure or use, and
>
> (ii) is the subject of efforts that are reasonable under the circumstances to maintain secrecy [2].

Almost any type of proprietary information may be kept as a trade secret, including technical data and specifications, as well as nontechnical data, plans, and business information, reports, and methods. Customer and client lists, business know-how, research results and studies, chemical formulae, production processes and methods or systems, and products such as computer hardware and software are eligible for protection. All such information can provide a competitive advantage and be of commercial use to the trade secret owner who keeps the information secret. Moreover, negative information, such as the results of unsuccessful experiments or inconclusive research or processes that are unworkable, can be protected as a trade secret. Such negative information is commercially valuable because it reveals those endeavors that are proven by experience or trial to be worthless or problematic [3].

The key to protection of a trade secret is, of course, secrecy. Proprietary information known by others or publicly available is not secret and not protectable. From a practical standpoint, absolute secrecy is not always required. In order to be useful in the business environment, a trade secret is often known by more individuals than its owner. However, the trade secret owner must take reasonable, affirmative steps to maintain the secrecy of the information sought to be protected. The owner's efforts to maintain secrecy must be reasonable within the context of the business and industry.

The sufficiency of the owner's efforts to maintain secrecy will be evaluated under the circumstances of each case. The courts will consider such factors as the extent to which the information is known by others within and outside of the business, the extent of precautions taken to guard the secrecy of the information, and the ease or difficulty with which the information could be properly acquired or independently replicated by others [4]. Reasonable efforts to maintain secrecy include "advising employees of the existence of a trade secret, limiting access to a trade secret on a 'need to know basis,' and controlling plant access. On the other hand, public disclosure of information through display, trade journal publication advertising, or other carelessness can preclude protection" [5].

Trade secret protection is not absolute and does not provide the owner with exclusive rights to the information. If a competitor is able to independently invent or discover the same information, then trade secret law is of no remedy. In addition, another may reverse engineer or disassemble the secret to determine how the technology was created or compiled. So long as the technology was obtained through lawful means, reverse engineering is not misappropriation. For instance, a product created by a secret process and sold on the mass market may be disassembled and studied by a competitor who properly purchased it to reveal the process used to create the product.

Trade secret misappropriation occurs when the secret is disclosed by someone in violation of a contractual duty to maintain its confidentiality, such as an employee or partner breaching a confidentiality agreement, or when the secret is obtained by another through improper means, such as a competitor gaining possession through theft or industrial espionage. When a trade secret has been misappropriated, its owner may sue to obtain an injunction to prevent or halt the misconduct. The trade secret owner may also recover damages for actual losses sustained as a result of the misappropriation. Where there is willful misappropriation, the owner may recover punitive damages as well [6].

A trade secret may be protected only as long as its owner prevents it from becoming common knowledge. Practically speaking, therefore, if the secret has already been disclosed, even though disclosure was improper or in breach of contract, an injunction against further disclosure may be of limited value. As such, although an injunction is often sought along with a request for monetary damages, the most useful remedy may be damages. Even if a court finds that there has been misappropriation, the proprietary information is no longer entitled to protection as a trade secret and any economic value that comes through its secrecy is lost forever.

Finally, the Economic Espionage Act (EEA) was enacted in 1996 to provide additional federal protection for trade secrets under certain circumstances. The statute makes it a federal crime to misappropriate trade secrets intending or knowing that doing so will benefit any foreign government or interest [7]. Any individual who violates the EEA may be imprisoned up to 15 years and/or be fined up to $500,000, whereas a corporation convicted under the statute may be fined up to $10 million [8]. The EEA provides a small measure of federal trade secret protection in the international marketplace, though in other countries, trade secrets are given greater or lesser protection. In addition, article 29 of the international Agreement on Trade-Related Aspects of Intellectual Property Rights (TRIPs) [9] requires that its signatories, which include most of the major industrialized trading nations, protect commercially valuable "undisclosed information" the use of which is restricted by reasonable measures to guarantee its secrecy.

Trade secrets and electronic information

As indicated earlier, once a trade secret is publicly disclosed, protection is lost and the trade secret owner may lose the right to enjoin others from using the secret, even if the secret is inadvertently revealed. For example, in *Unix Sys. Labs. v. Berkeley Software Design, Inc.* [10], a software licensee unintentionally disclosed Unix source code by allowing subscribers to an electronic bulletin board to download software containing the source code. In *Religious Technology Center v. F.A.C.T.Net, Inc.* [11], the Church of Scientology sued several former members for trade secret misappropriation for copying Church documents that they subsequently posted on the Internet. The court denied the Church's request for injunctive relief. The court held that the documents had lost their trade secret status when they were made publicly available on the Internet during an earlier court proceeding [12].

Nevertheless, in the case of *DVD Copy Control Association, Inc. v. McLaughlin* [13], the court issued a preliminary injunction barring Internet disclosure of a proprietary encryption system for protecting DVDs, despite the court's admission that the trade secret had been posted and widely available on the Internet for some time and that enforcement of the injunction outside of the jurisdiction might prove to be impossible. Such a holding is probably more of an anomaly than the likely result in most cases involving similar circumstances.

Additionally, trade secret law does not protect against independent discovery or invention by a competitor. Thus, it is possible for more than one business to autonomously develop the same process or program, and neither may use trade secret law to claim an exclusive right over it. Likewise, trade secret law does not provide relief against reverse engineering. Thus, a competitor may lawfully acquire, inspect, and disassemble a copy of a program and use the information for its own purposes. The key here is that the competitor must have acquired the information through honest and fair means before reverse engineering it. If the information was acquired by improper or unlawful means before being reverse engineered, the trade secret has been misappropriated.

For instance, in *Data General Corp. v. Digital Computer Controls, Inc.* [14], a defendant that had lawfully acquired hardware, but had discovered the trade secret using confidential documents that it had improperly obtained, could not then escape liability by claiming that it had reverse engineered the hardware. By contrast, the defendant in *University Computing Co. v. Lykes-Youngstown Corp.* [15] was found to have misappropriated trade secret–protected software when the defendant obtained a copy of the software by bribing an employee of one of the trade secret owner's customers.

The existence of a confidential relationship will also give rise to situations in which trade secrets may be misappropriated. In the business environment, a confidential relationship may arise between employers and employees or between partners to a joint venture. Trade secrets that are disclosed within the context of a confidential relationship can be protected in several ways. The courts will not often imply a duty not to disclose unless there has been notice that the information is secret.

Typically, the trade secret owner uses a contract in the form of a nondisclosure or a noncompetition agreement to ensure that the information remains confidential. If the employee or partner later uses or reveals the information, the trade secret owner may sue for misappropriation and breach of contract. The court in *Integrated Cash Mgmt. Servs., Inc. v. Digital Transactions, Inc.* [16], found that a former employee, who had signed a nondisclosure agreement and later developed competing software after leaving his position, had misappropriated his former employer's trade secret. The court explained: "The existence of a nondisclosure agreement puts the employee on notice that the programs are considered trade secrets" [17].

The importance of a confidentiality agreement or special relationship between a trade secret owner and another who is accused of misappropriating the secret was recently underscored in *Ford Motor Co. v. Lane* [18]. In that case, the defendant acquired possession of documents containing confidential information about Ford Motor Company and its products. The defendant threatened to and later published a number of these newsworthy documents on a Web site he maintained. He claimed that he was unaware of the identity of the individuals who delivered these materials to him, though the court surmised that they were former and current Ford employees under a duty to keep such materials confidential. Ford then sued for trade secret misappropriation and sought to enjoin further publication of these materials. In denying the plaintiff's request, the court held that even though Ford had proved that it was likely that the defendant had misappropriated the trade secrets, enjoining his conduct would constitute an unconstitutional prior restraint on speech proscribed by the First Amendment: "In the absence of a confidentiality agreement or fiduciary duty between the parties, Ford's commercial interest in its trade secrets and [defendant's] alleged improper conduct in obtaining the trade secrets are not grounds for issuing a prior restraint" [19].

As to noncompetition agreements (sometimes referred to as restrictive covenants) by which an employee agrees not to compete against a former employer, they are enforceable if they contain substantively reasonable terms. The restraint must apply only to the trade secret and must be limited as to its duration and geographic scope. Thus, a noncompetition agreement that lasts in perpetuity and prohibits competition across a very broad geographic area would be unenforceable as unreasonable.

The nature of electronic commerce may be increasingly relevant in evaluating the reasonableness of a noncompetition agreement. In *EarthWeb, Inc. v. Schlack* [20], for instance, EarthWeb sued for a preliminary injunction to prevent a former vice president from either working for, or disclosing trade secrets to, a competitor. Such relief was mandated, claimed the plaintiff, by a one-year restrictive covenant in the defendant's employment agreement. Nevertheless, the court held that this provision was not enforceable because, given the nature of the Internet today, it interfered with defendant's employment for an unreasonably long period of time [21]. Stated the court: "[T]he one-year duration of EarthWeb's restrictive covenant is too long given the dynamic nature of this industry, its lack of geographic borders, and Schlack's former cutting-edge position with EarthWeb where his success depended on keeping abreast of daily changes in content on the Internet" [22].

Also noteworthy concerning this case was that EarthWeb's claim was based on the doctrine of inevitable disclosure, which permits an employer to enjoin an employee from accepting a job with a competitor, where the nature of the work will inevitably lead the employee to reveal or use the former employer's trade secrets. The court was reluctant to invoke this rule without evidence of actual misappropriation by Schlack, which was not present on the facts of the case [23]. However, the court in another case, *Doubleclick, Inc. v. Henderson* [24], applied the inevitable disclosure doctrine to bar two former Doubleclick employees from starting their own Web advertising firm for six months.

With respect to electronic databases and software distributed on-line, the question arises regarding how best to maintain confidentiality. The most commonly used method of doing this is the on-line "shrinkwrap" or "clickwrap" license agreement, which can be used to restrict disclosure of trade secret information or data, or prohibit reverse engineering or decompilation. For instance, the court in *Telerate Sys., Inc. v. Caro.* [25], enforced a software license that contained a nondisclosure provision against a customer who had licensed an on-line database. When there is a nondisclosure agreement in place, its breach or violation will be proof of misappropriation.

In addition, proof of misappropriation may be found in the substantial similarity of design or code, which creates an inference that the trade secret was stolen, copied without permission, or wrongfully used. In *Dynamic Research Co. v. Analytical Sciences Corp.* [26], for instance, the court found no misappropriation by a former employee who had developed a competing computer program because the data structures of the competing program differed significantly from those of the secret program. Likewise, the court in *SOS, Inc. v. Payday, Inc.* [27], held that a license granting remote access to a payroll program did not preclude a finding of misappropriation when the licensee made a copy of the program and began using the trade secret information contained in the software.

Protecting trade secrets in the digital environment

As this discussion suggests, an important aspect of trade secret protection is the extent to which the owner undertook reasonable efforts to maintain secrecy through internal and external security measures. The following checklist summarizes the measures that a business should consider when implementing a program to maintain the confidentiality of its proprietary electronic information:

- Notify employees that the information is confidential (in a nondisclosure agreement, noncompetition agreement, and employment contract) and instruct them on how to use the information in their work in order to maintain its secrecy.
- Require joint venture partners and employees to sign nondisclosure agreements (aside from any provisions that also appear in an employment contract or partnership or joint venture agreement) and remind them of their ongoing duty of confidentiality at their exit interviews or termination of the venture.
- Use nondisclosure agreements to protect against disclosure of trade secrets revealed during negotiations with potential partners, employees, and customers.
- Impose internal physical security measures and procedures, including locks; security checkpoints; video and electronic monitoring; log-in procedures, passwords, intranets, and firewalls; restricted access areas; encryption of stored data; logging use and access of databases and programs; notices and signs; destruction of discarded hard copy documents and print-outs; among others.
- Clearly mark or label all protected information as "confidential," "secret" or "proprietary."
- Limit access to only those individuals who must use the information.
- Restrict or prohibit distribution or publication of confidential information at trade shows, demonstrations, and in academic journals or conferences, and review all material to be released to the public to ensure that no trade secrets are revealed.

- Distribute only object code rather than source code when the trade secret is a computer program, and use copy protection systems for safeguarding such code.
- Encrypt trade secret data or code when distributing or transmitting it on-line to prevent disclosure through unauthorized interception.

Trade secret protection will remain a valuable tool by which to secure and maintain a competitive advantage in the information economy. As such, the development and effective enforcement of a monitoring and use program will be increasingly important when trade secrets take the form of electronic data and information technology.

Endnotes

[1] This is one distinction from patent and copyright law, which are exclusively governed by federal law and which entail formal application and registration procedures. The subject matter protected by patent and copyright law, as well as the duration of protection, rights, and remedies provided by these alternative forms of protection, also differ considerably. For a discussion of these differences and their advantages and disadvantages compared to trade secret law, see Pooley, J. and W. Bratic, "The Value of Trade Secrets," *Managing Intellectual Property,* October 1999, pp. 66–69.

[2] Uniform Trade Secrets Act (USTA) § 1(4). In those states that have not adopted this act, the common law of trade secrets applies. The Restatement of Torts § 757 cmt. b, which summarizes the applicable common law, defines a trade secret as "any formula, pattern, device or compilation of information which is used in one's business. And gives him an opportunity to obtain an advantage over competitors who do not know or use it ...." This definition is virtually identical to that of the USTA.

[3] As one court described it, "Knowing what not to do often leads automatically to knowing what to do." *Metallurgical Indus., Inc. v. Fourtek, Inc.*, 790 F.2d 1195, 1203 (5th Cir. 1986).

[4] *See* Restatement of Torts § 757 cmt. b.

[5] UTSA § 1 cmt.

[6] Punitive damages, also referred to as exemplary damages, are additional money damages above actual loss suffered that may be imposed as a punishment for malicious or willful misappropriation or misconduct.

[7] 18 U.S.C. §§ 1831–39.

[8] See *U.S. v. Hsu*, 155 F.3d 189 (3d Cir. 1998)(applying the criminal provisions of the EEA).

[9] Trade-Related Aspects of Intellectual Property, Final Act Embodying the Results of the Uruguay Round of the Multilateral Trade Negotiations, Dec. 15, 1993, www.wto.org/english/docs_e/docs_e.htm.

[10] 27 U.S.P.Q.2d 1721 (D.N.J. 1993).

[11] 901 F. Supp. 1519 (D. Colo. 1995).

[12] *See Religious Tech. Ctr. v. Netcome On-Line.com*, 923 F. Supp. 1231 (N.D. Cal. 1995); *Religious Tech. Ctr. v. Lerma*, 908 F. Supp. 1362 (E.D. Va. 1995).

[13] No. 786804 (Cal. Sup. Ct. 2000).

[14] 357 A.2d 105 (Del. Ch. 1981).

[15] 504 F.2d 518 (5th Cir. 1974).

[16] 732 F. Supp. 370 (S.D.N.Y. 1989).

[17] *Id.*

[18] No. 99-74205, 1999 U.S. Dist. Lexis 13736 (E.D. Mich., Sept. 7, 1999).

[19] *Id.*

[20] 99 Civ. 10035 (WHP), 1999 WL 980165 (S.D.N.Y., Oct. 27, 1999).

[21] Employment in e-businesses and the information technology market is characterized by high turnover rates. Many businesses are now requiring employees at all levels, including nontechnical support and clerical employees, to sign confidentiality agreements. See Lewis, D. E., "Keeping a Lock on Intellectual Property," May 19, 2000, http://www.digitalmass.com/news/daily/05/19/ip_law.html.

[22] *Id.*

[23] *Id.*

[24] No. 11691, 1997 WL 731413 (N.Y. Sup. Ct. 1997).

[25] 8 USPQ2d 1740 (S.D.N.Y. 1988).

[26] 400 N.E.2d 1274 (Mass. App. Ct. 1980).

[27] 886 F.2d 1018 (9th Cir. 1989).

5

Protecting trademarks on the Internet

A trademark identifies a product's origin or source and helps consumers distinguish one brand from another. A trademark is a valuable commercial asset that protects the goodwill of a business and that can be used on-line. Use of trademarks in electronic commerce raises several important issues regarding the scope of trademark protection. As businesses seek to create a presence on the Internet, it becomes increasingly important to understand and protect the rights afforded by trademark registration. To avoid becoming either a victim or a defendant in a lawsuit, businesses must be vigilant about their trademarks and careful in using others' trademarks on the Internet. This chapter examines the nature of trademarks and considers several key legal issues concerning their use in the on-line marketplace.

Requirements for trademark protection

A trademark is "any word, name, symbol, or device, or any combination thereof...used...to identify and distinguish...goods...from those manufactured or sold by others and to indicate the source of the goods" [1]. A trademark serves as a reassurance of quality to consumers, allowing them to associate it with a product. In addition, trademarks can be protected through federal registration with the United States Patent and Trademark Office (USPTO). Most states provide for their own registration of trademarks, but because trademarks used on the Internet are transmitted in interstate and international commerce, state registration is not an effective form of protection in this environment. Federal registration of a trademark provides the owner with legal rights and remedies against those who use the trademark without permission.

Trademarks are classified in the order of their increasing distinctiveness: generic, descriptive, suggestive, arbitrary, and fanciful. The more distinctive the mark, the greater the protection afforded by law [2]. Generic marks, which define or are synonymous with particular products, can never be protected [3]. A mark such as "Breakfast Cereal" adopted for a breakfast food is considered generic. However, a unique trademark such as Kleenex or Xerox may become generic if it works its way into everyday speech so as to lose its distinctiveness. To prevent this, businesses often guard their trademarks by bringing or threatening infringement actions any time the mark is used in a generic manner.

Suggestive marks are considered distinctive because they engage the consumer's imagination in determining the product source. As an example, "Westlaw" is suggestive because it links the legal research software with its source, The West Group. Fanciful and arbitrary marks are considered inherently distinctive. Made-up words like "Exxon" or "Electrolux" are examples of fanciful trademarks. Arbitrary marks are real words assigned to products where there is no connection between the word and the product. "Apple Computer" or "Sun Microsystems" are examples of arbitrary trademarks. Descriptive marks, which describe the type of qualities of the product, are not inherently distinctive. They may, however, become distinctive when they acquire a secondary meaning, allowing them to represent a particular source in the minds of consumers. To determine if a descriptive mark has a secondary meaning, courts consider the

- Length and manner of use;
- Nature and extent of advertising and promotion;
- Efforts made to promote conscious connection in the public's mind between the trademark and the business;

- Extent to which the public actually identifies the mark and the product or service, as measured by consumer surveys.

If a combination of these factors has led consumers to associate the mark with the product, then it has acquired secondary meaning. Examples of such marks are "U-Haul" and "International Business Machines."

Trademark rights are tied to geographic location. The actual and possible geographic market for the product or service, and the extent of advertising, may limit claims for the improper use of the mark. In fact, the same mark may be separately owned in different countries. The Internet, however, greatly enlarges the scope of a possible market as it is worldwide. At present, there exists no international trademark registration agency; however, article 16(1) of the General Agreement on Trade and Tariffs on Trade-Related Aspects of Intellectual Property Rights provides for cross-recognition and protection of the trademarks registered by signatory countries. In addition, the Paris Convention for the Protection of Industrial Property, to which the United States adheres, requires its signatories to treat citizens of other signatories the same for purposes of registration, but does not require recognition of a foreign trademark.

Trademark infringement and dilution

Under federal law, trademark owners are entitled to protection from the improper use of their marks through infringement and dilution. The Lanham Trademark Act [4] forbids the commercial use of a federally registered mark without permission when that use is likely to cause confusion in the minds of consumers. Infringement occurs when the use of a mark by one person creates a likelihood of confusion with the mark of another in the minds of consumers. To determine the likelihood of confusion, the courts will examine several factors, including the:

- Similarity of the marks;
- Similarity of the goods or services;
- Character of the market;
- Strength of the mark;
- Intent of the alleged infringer.

Ultimately, the concern is with the effect of the similarity on actual or potential consumers. In the case of *Playboy Enterprises, Inc. v. Frena* [5], Playboy sued Frena, the operator of an electronic bulletin board service, where subscribers often uploaded and downloaded copies of Playboy photographs for exchange. Playboy's registered "Playboy" and "Playmate" trademarks appeared on many of the images. Although Frena claimed that he could not regulate what his subscribers placed on the bulletin board, the court held that this amounted to infringement: "It is likely that customers of Defendant Frena would believe that [Playboy] was the source of Defendant Frena's images and that [Playboy] either sponsored, endorsed, or approved [his] use of the images" [6]. The owner of the trademark may seek an injunction against an infringer, recover monetary damages, or both [7].

In addition, the Federal Trademark Dilution Act [8] creates a federal claim for dilution of famous trademarks. Dilution occurs when, through the use of a similar or identical mark, a strong and well-known registered trademark is weakened as a means of identifying and distinguishing a particular product or service. To determine whether a mark is famous, courts will consider such factors as:

- The degree of inherent or acquired distinctiveness of the mark;
- The extent to which the mark is used with the sale of the product or service;
- The extent of advertising and publicity of the mark;
- The size of geographical area in which the mark is used;
- The channels of trade for the product or service;
- The degree of the mark's recognition;
- The extent to which the same or similar marks are used by others;
- Whether the mark is federally registered.

Unlike infringement, dilution can occur without any competitive relationship between the parties and without confusion as to source. Instead, the Trademark Dilution Act is designed to remedy the harm suffered when the distinctive reputation and marketing value of a mark as a source of identification and quality is blurred or tarnished by use on noncompeting products or services. Blurring occurs over a period of time when the mark is used with unrelated products to the point that its identification with the trademark owner is whittled away, for example: "Kodak" pianos, "Buick" aspirin, or "DuPont" shoes. Tarnishment results when the mark is used with some unsavory product, causing a loss of reputation or consumer goodwill. The owner of a famous mark may seek an injunction against a person who "willfully intended to trade on the owner's reputation or cause dilution of the famous mark" [9].

Trademark rights and hypermedia

Hypertext Markup Language (HTML) is the main computer programming language used to create sites on the World Wide Web for display by an Internet browser such as Netscape Communicator or Microsoft Explorer. The HTML coding is not visible to the viewer; rather, the text and graphical images and the manner in which they have been arranged by the code is what appears when a Web page is displayed. For example, to display the subtitle to this section on a Web page as it appears above, the following HTML coding would be used:

```
<HEAD>

<TITLE>Trademark Rights and Hypermedia<TITLE>

<HEAD>
```

The enormous quantity and variety of information on the Web makes it useful for businesses to use tools like hypertext links, frames, and meta-tags to assist consumers in finding their sites and related information.

Linking

Hypertext links, or links, allow Web site owners to connect their sites to sites containing related information. These links are constructed using HTML and may appear as underlined text or as graphical images. When a viewer of a Web site containing a hypertext link points the mouse and clicks on the link, he or she is electronically and instantaneously transported to another linked Web site. Although hyperlinks can function as footnotes or endnotes, linking to a Web site by way of a trademark could infringe or dilute the mark contained on the linked site. The display by a Web site owner of another business' trademark that links to the trademark owner's home page may imply a commercial relationship with that business. Similarly, the instantaneous transition between displays of linked materials may be confusing to viewers, who might easily lose track of their electronic location within layers of hyperlinks and Web site pages. The viewers may reach the mistaken conclusion that all linked materials originate from the same source. Thus, instead of viewing hyperlinks as a means of transportation from one site to the next, viewers may believe they are traveling within one site.

In the case of *Ticketmaster Corp. v. Microsoft Corp.* [10], Ticketmaster, a seller of tickets to concerts and other events, sued Microsoft Corp. for hyperlinking to Microsoft's "Seattle Sidewalk" city guide Web site, the ticket sales page of Ticketmaster's site containing its trademark, without Ticketmaster's authorization. By doing this and bypassing Ticketmaster's home page by deep linking, Ticketmaster alleged, among other claims, that the Microsoft hyperlinks were diluting Ticketmaster's trademarks and diverting viewers away from the rest of its Web site. Microsoft responded that "any business, such as Ticketmaster, participating in the Internet and the World Wide Web invites other participants to use the business' Internet addresses and URLs to contact it..." [11]. The parties in this case eventually settled when Microsoft agreed to remove its deep links [12].

Framing

Closely related to linking is a device known as framing. Framing allows the viewer to click on a hyperlink, which then displays within a bordered frame on the Web site being viewed, material that is located on another Web site under another URL. This practice has led to lawsuits alleging that framing may dilute or infringe trademarks displayed within the frame because it may create the impression that the framed content is part of the Web site on which the frame appears or has been authorized by the content provider.

In the case of *Washington Post Co. v. TotalNews, Inc.* [13], TotalNews displayed the content and trademarked logos from various news provider sites within a frame on the TotalNews site. *The Washington Post* and several other news providers whose content had been framed by TotalNews claimed that TotalNews, Inc. had "designed a parasite website that republishes the news and editorial content of others' websites in order to attract both advertisers and users." Among other claims, the news providers brought claims for trademark dilution and infringement. Eventually, the case was settled with an agreement by which TotalNews was allowed to continue to link to the news providers' sites, but only in such a way that the content of the news providers' sites does not appear in a frame within the display of the TotalNews Web site.

The outcome in the *TotalNews* litigation did little to clarify the questions surrounding framing. Some of those questions were raised again in *Futuredontics, Inc. v. Applied Anagramatics, Inc.* [14]. Futuredontics, the owner of a Web site advertising its dental referral service, discovered that the defendant's site was framing material from Futuredontics' Web site, including Futuredontics' registered service mark. The defendant's frame included its own logo and service information, but failed to properly reference the plaintiff. Futuredontics sued for trademark and copyright infringement, and Applied Anagramatics moved to dismiss the case and arrive at judgment on the pleadings, with respect to the copyright claim. The court denied these motions and the lawsuit has proceeded. This case indicates that there is a potential claim when a frame misrepresents the source of the framed Web page.

Metatagging

A final area of concern involves metatags, which are used to designate words that are written in HTML and identifiable to search engines, some of which are not visible to the eye. Search engines index certain selected keywords appearing in the HTML version of the Web site document and use the first words found in the document as an abstract to direct a consumer to the site. The author of the Web site can use metatags to control how the search engine will index the site by including additional keywords to index as well as a brief description.

This device can be misused by one business to hide the trademark of a popular competitor in the Web site metatags so that a viewer searching for the competitor by name will find the first business' site as well. One court dealt with this practice in the case of *Playboy Enterprises, Inc. v. Calvin Designer Label* [15], where the defendant's Web sites contained the PLAYMATE or PLAYBOY trademarks and these terms were buried as metatags in the Web site's HTML code. Playboy discovered this practice when a potential customer who was seeking its Web site, using the term "Playboy" in a search engine, was referred to the defendant's *Playmate Live*

Magazine site instead. The court enjoined this practice, concluding that the designer's use of Playboy's trademarks likely violated trademark law [16].

On the other hand, there is a way in which Web site owners may properly incorporate another business' trademarks into their site's metatags. The trademark fair use defense played an important role in *Playboy Enterprises, Inc. v. Welles* [17]. A business may fairly use a competitor's mark without facing liability if it is used not as a trademark, but instead to, in good faith, describe one's goods or services [18]. Fair use permits businesses to use a protected mark to describe aspects of their own goods [19]. Additionally, the act permits use of another's famous mark in comparative advertising to identify the competing goods or services of the famous mark's owner [20].

In the *Welles* case, former Playboy Playmate Terri Welles established a Web site that contained photographs of herself and other information. The Web site included the heading, "Terri Welles—Playmate of the Year 1981," as well as the terms "Playmate," " Playboy," and "Playmate of the Year" as metatags. Welles also included a disclaimer on the Web site that read: "This site is neither endorsed, nor sponsored by, nor affiliated with Playboy Enterprises, Inc. PLAYBOY, PLAYMATE OF THE YEAR and PLAYMATE OF THE MONTH are registered trademarks of Playboy Enterprises, Inc." Nevertheless, Playboy sued Welles for trademark infringement and dilution and sought to enjoin her from using its trademarks in her Web site metatags and Web site background. The court, however, ruled that Welles' use of Playboy's trademarks were fair use because

> it is evident that Ms. Welles has minimized her references to *Playboy* on her website and has not attempted to trick consumers into believing that they are viewing a Playboy-endorsed website.... It is clear that defendant is selling Terri Welles and only Terri Welles on the Web site. There is no overt attempt to confuse the websurfer into believing that her site is a Playboy-related website. In this case, then, defendant's use of the term Playmate of the Year 1981 "is descriptive of and used fairly and in good faith only to describe [herself]" [21].

Regarding the metatags specifically, the court added that there was "no trademark infringement where the defendant has used the plaintiff's trademarks in good faith to index the content of her website" and that "use of the term Playboy is not an infringement because it references not only her identity as a '*Playboy* Playmate of the Year 1981,' but it may also reference legitimate editorial uses of the term…" [22].

More recently, a federal appellate court addressed the metatagging issue in the case of *Brookfield Communications, Inc. v. West Coast Entertainment Corp.* [23]. Brookfield gathers and sells information about the entertainment industry and uses the federally registered mark, "moviebuff.com," for its software. Brookfield discovered that West Coast, one of the nation's largest video rental store chains, intended to launch a Web site as moviebuff.com. West Coast planned for its site to contain a searchable entertainment base similar to the plaintiffs and to use the trademarked term in its metatags and domain name. West Coast had registered moviebuff.com with domain name registrar Network Solutions before Brookfield had filed for its trademark registration. Brookfield sued, and when its request for a preliminary injunction was denied, it appealed.

The Ninth Circuit entered an order enjoining West Coast from using or facilitating the use in any manner, including advertising promotion, the mark "moviebuff" or any other term or terms likely to cause confusion, including moviebuff.com. The court noted that the .com marks were ordinarily used with the company's name, and were normally in metatags used by search engines to locate the company:

> Using another's trademark in one's meta tags is much like posting a sign with another's trademark in front of one's store. Suppose West Coast's competitor (let's call it Blockbuster) puts up a billboard on a highway reading "West Coast Video: 2 miles ahead at Exit 7" – where West Coast is really located at Exit 8 but Blockbuster is located at Exit 7. Customers looking for West Coast's store will pull off at Exit 7 and drive around looking for it. Unable to locate West Coast, but seeing the Blockbuster store right by the highway entrance, they may simply rent there. Even consumers who prefer West Coast might find it not worth the trouble to continue searching for West Coast since there is a Blockbuster store right there [24].

The court added, however, that if a Web site had merely compared its goods to a competitor's, the Web site's inclusion of the competitor's trademark in its metatags would constitute fair use [25].

Keyword advertising

On-line advertising has raised another interesting trademark issue. Banner advertisements, which appear at the top of many commercial Web sites, allow the user to click on the ad and be transported directly to the home page of the advertiser, or to other relevant content regarding an offer. Some Internet search engine sites sell keyword ads, whereby the search engine displays an advertiser's banner ads in random rotation on Web pages containing the search results. For an increased fee, the search engine will display an advertiser's banner ads whenever a user types in one of a series of designated terms in his search. This practice allows the advertiser to target his ads and reach a more receptive audience.

Some advertisers pay to have their ads appear on the page displaying results from a search that used another's trademark as the query term. For instance, suppose a seller of computers wanted to advertise its computers on-line using banner advertising. The seller would contact a search engine service and, in addition to buying keywords such as "hardware" or "computer," might buy "Compaq" or "Dell" as keywords. When someone conducts a search using "Dell" as a keyword, the computer seller's banner ad will appear at the top of the search results page. The person might be tempted to click on the banner ad and later purchase a computer from the seller rather than Dell.

Whether this practice creates a likelihood of confusion that leads to trademark infringement was the issue that arose in *Playboy Enterprises, Inc. v. Netscape Communications Corp.* [26]. In this case, Playboy brought suit to challenge Netscape's keying of advertisements on its Excite search engine to the terms "playboy" and "playmate," which are Playboy's registered trademarks. As a result of a search using one or more of these terms, users are provided not only with a list of Web sites that contain the word "playboy" or "playmate," but also by a paid banner advertisement from a seller of adult entertainment services. Although the banner ads did not contain either the word "playboy" or "playmate," Playboy argued that this practice was trademark infringement and dilution.

The court disagreed, and found that Playboy's claims failed because Playboy did not show that consumers were likely to be confused by Netscape's use of Playboy's mark. Playboy offered no evidence showing that consumers believed that the banner advertisements shown when they conducted their search for the term "playboy" were affiliated with, or endorsed by Playboy. The court also noted that the search results produced in response to a "playboy" search contained not only a banner ad but links to Playboy's Web sites as well. Moreover, the court held that Netscape's use of "playboy" and "playmate" in keying was a permissible, fair use of Playboy's marks and was protected by the First Amendment.

> Here, [Playboy] is seeking to leverage its trademarks "Playboy(R)" and "Playmate(R)" (which cannot be searched on the Internet) into a monopoly on the words "playboy" and "playmate". Indeed, by seeking a prohibition on all advertisements that appear in response to the search words "playboy" and "playmate," [Playboy] would effectively monopolize the use of these words on the Internet. This violates the First Amendment rights of (a) Excite and Netscape; (b) other trademark holders of "playboy" and "playmate"; as well as (c) members of the public who conduct Internet searches [27].

The result in this case may foreshadow how other courts will respond to challenges to keyword advertising. On the other hand, there may be other on-line advertising practices developed in the future that make use of trademarks and that will amount to trademark infringement or dilution. Regardless of the court's decision in the *Playboy* case, businesses should attempt to determine whether their competitors are exploiting their trademarks and whether these practices are causing consumer confusion or dilution.

Trademark rights and domain names

Domain names function as an alphanumeric address system for the Internet, allowing consumers to identify and locate particular businesses in much the same way as a street address or telephone number. As the number of people who have access to the Internet grows rapidly each year, domain names are emerging as an increasingly valuable tool for businesses to attract and inform potential consumers about their products and services. Consequently, domain names are becoming increasingly important business assets in much the same manner as trademarks. Indeed, some domain names may incorporate or function essentially as trademarks. In those instances, important questions arise about the extent of protection afforded by trademark law.

A domain name identifies the location and category of a particular Web site. The domain name united.com, for example, contains a top-level and second-level name. There are seven top-level domain names: .edu for educational institutions; .com for commercial businesses; .org for noncommercial organizations; .int for noncommercial international organizations; .net for network gateways; .gov for governmental offices; and .mil for the military. Second-level names, such as "united," are more specific identifiers and exist within top-level domains.

The United States National Science Foundation (NSF) created the International Network Information Center (InterNIC) to serve as the central information source for the Internet. The NSF then contracted with Network Solutions, Inc. (NSI), a private firm, to assign and register domain names. In 1998, the Internet Corporation for Assigned Names and Numbers (ICANN), a private nonprofit corporation assumed responsibility for designating registrars of domain names. There are now several domain name registrars. To become accessible on the Internet, a business must have an Internet protocol address and obtain and register a domain name. Domain names are assigned on a first-come, first-served basis, and only one domain name per business may be registered. NSI, for instance, does not investigate to determine if a requested domain name incorporates or violates a registered trademark; instead, the applicant has the responsibility to do so. Under NSI's policy, applicants must confirm that

- The applicant's statements in the application are true and that the applicant has the right to use the domain name requested;
- The applicant has a bona fide intention to regularly use the domain name;
- The registration and use of the name does not interfere with or infringe the intellectual property right of any other party in any jurisdiction;
- The applicant is not seeking to use the name for any unlawful purpose, including unfair competition.

The applicant must agree to indemnify NSI against all disputes arising from the use or registration of the domain name. NSI does not arbitrate or adjudicate trademark disputes involving domain names. Instead, when a dispute arises, NSI will put the domain name on hold pending the dispute's resolution [28]. As to the process of resolving domain name disputes, ICANN has adopted an arbitration procedure that its domain name registrars now follow. This procedure is discussed more fully below. Moreover, in 2000, ICANN approved for general use the new top-level domains .biz for businesses, .name for individuals, .museum for museums, .coop for business cooperatives, and .aero for the aviation industry. The new top-level domain names are intended to address the shortage of name choices now available for the .com, .org, and .net domains, due to their popularity with businesses.

Domain name registration, unlike trademark registration, does not vest any rights of ownership in the domain name since it can be revoked. A problem arises when one business' domain name contains words constituting another business' trademark. Although no law expressly prohibits this, there may be consumer confusion as to the origin of the product or service, which constitutes infringement under the federal Lanham Trademark Act. Another infringement problem arises when someone requests a domain name, intending it to be confusingly similar to another's product or service, with the hope that it can be sold at a profit.

Similarly, a number of issues emerge when assessing the usefulness of applying trademark law to domain names. For instance, does or should the initial registrations of a domain name containing a trademark in itself constitute infringement or dilution? Trademark law permits registration of the identical names for noncompeting goods and services, but only one domain name using that same name can be registered by NSI. For instance, trademarks such as United Air, United Shoe, and United Van Lines can coexist, but there can be but one united.com domain name. Another difficulty is the lack of geographic and product or service differentiation in Internet addresses. For example, the domain name aaa.com could identify the on-line address of the American Automobile Association or the American Arbitration Association even though consumers could easily distinguish between the services provided by each.

There are some parallels between domain names and existing categories of protectable trademarks. One analogy, for instance, is to geographic location names; however, geographic location names generally are treated as addresses, which are merely descriptive of a particular locale. Trademark protection does not extend unless they have acquired secondary meaning. Another analogy is to television or radio broadcast station call letters, which can be registered and enforced as trademarks by the prior user.

Likewise, there may be an analogy to vanity telephone numbers used as pseudonyms. These are usually protectable, though purely generic alphanumeric terms or phrases are not [29].

In an early trademark dispute involving a domain name, Princeton Review registered the domain name kaplan.com and established an Internet site under that name. Stanley Kaplan Review is Princeton Review's arch-competitor in the standardized test preparation market. By doing this, Princeton Review prevented Kaplan from registering its own trademark as its domain name. Kaplan sued and demanded that Princeton Review cease its use of the name. The suit was settled by arbitration, which led to Princeton Review's surrender of the domain name. Another case involved a *Wired* magazine writer, Joshua Quittner, who registered the name mcdonalds.com. The dispute was resolved when McDonald's agreed to underwrite the purchase of computer equipment for a local grade school in exchange for the rights to the domain name [30].

More recently, in the case of *Intermatic Inc., v. Toeppen* [31], Intermatic alleged that Toeppen infringed its trademark when he registered and used the domain name intermatic.com. The federal court reserved the infringement claim for trial to determine if there was consumer confusion, but held that the federal Trademark Dilution Act and the Illinois Anti-Dilution Act had been violated. According to the court:

> Toeppen's conduct has caused dilution in at least two respects. First, Toeppen's registration of the intermatic.com domain name lessens the capacity of Intermatic to identify and distinguish its goods and services by means of the Internet. Intermatic is not currently free to use its mark as its domain name.... Such conduct lessens the capacity of Intermatic to identify its goods to potential consumers who would expect to locate Intermatic on the Internet through the "intermatic.com" domain name.... Second, Toeppen's conduct dilutes the Intermatic mark by using the Intermatic mark on its web page.... Dilution of Intermatic's mark is likely to occur because the domain name appears on the web page and is included on every page that is printed from the web page [32].

Likewise, in *Panavision International v. Toeppen* [33], the court applied the Trademark Dilution Act to another domain name dispute. Toeppen had registered domain names for Panavision, Delta Airlines, Neiman Marcus, Eddie Bauer, Lufthansa, among others. He had already attempted to sell the domain name intermatic.com to Intermatic, Inc. for $10,000 and americanstandard.com to American Standard, Inc. for $15,000. Panavision sued Toeppen, claiming he had diluted its trademark. Toeppen did not dispute that the Panavision mark was famous, that he began to use the mark after it became famous, or that he used the mark in commerce. Instead, Toeppen argued that he did not make commercial use of the mark and that his use of the mark did not dilute its quality.

The court agreed that merely registering Panavision's trademark as his domain name did not constitute a commercial use [34]; however, the court found that Toeppen operated a business that involved registering trademarks as domain names and then selling them to the registered trademark owners. Thus, the court concluded that this was indeed a commercial use. As such, the court concluded that Toeppen's use of Panavision's trademark as his domain name diluted the mark.

The Anticybersquatting Consumer Protection Act

To provide an additional federal remedy for cybersquatting, Congress enacted the Anticybersquatting Consumer Protection Act (ACPA). The ACPA provides:

> A person shall be liable in a civil action by the owner of a mark, including a personal name which is protected as a mark under this section, if, without regard to the goods or services of the parties, that person –
>
> (i) has a bad faith intent to profit from that mark, including a personal name which is protected as a mark under this section; and
>
> (ii) registers, traffics in, or uses a domain name that –
>
> > (I) in the case of a mark that is distinctive at the time of registration of the domain name, is identical or confusingly similar to that mark;
> >
> > (II) in the case of a famous mark that is famous at the time of registration of the domain name, is identical or confusingly similar to or dilutive of that mark... [35].

The ACPA further states that "a court may order the forfeiture or cancellation of the domain name or the transfer of the domain name to the owner of the mark," and provides that damages can be awarded for violations of the act [36].

The case of *Sporty's Farm LLC v. Sportsman's Market, Inc.* [37], was the first dispute in which a court interpreted and applied the ACPA. Sportsman's Market, Inc. was the owner of the federally registered trademark "Sporty's," which it has used since at least 1985 in the operation of its mail order catalog business. Omega Engineering, Inc. was a mail order catalog company that sells scientific process measurement instruments. In late 1994 or early 1995, Omega decided to enter into competition with Sportsman's, and registered the domain name sportys.com with NSI. Omega then formed a wholly owned subsidiary, Sporty's Farm (SF), and sold its rights to the sportys.com domain name to SF.

In March of 1996, Sportsman's discovered that Omega had registered the sportys.com domain and in the lawsuit that followed, Sportsman's claimed that Omega and SF had infringed and diluted its trademark. The court determined that the plaintiff had violated the ACPA because SF had used Sportsman's mark in the domain name it registered with a "bad faith intent to profit" thereby. In reaching this result, the court considered the nine factors set forth in the statute for determining if the party in question acted in bad faith. The court observed that Omega had decided to enter into competition with the defendant, and that it then registered a domain name that contained what it knew to be the defendant's mark, which had no relation to Omega's business. Based on these facts, the court concluded that "it cannot be doubted...that Omega registered sportys.com for the primary purpose of keeping Sportsman's from using that domain name" [38].

In a subsequent case, *Virtual Works, Inc. v. Volkswagen of America, Inc., et al.* [39], the Fourth Circuit Court of Appeals, affirmed a determination that Virtual Works had violated the ACPA by registering and then offering to sell to Volkswagen the domain name vw.net, which contains defendant Volkswagen's famous "vw" mark. The court determined, based on the evidence, that Virtual Works had an ulterior purpose in selecting the vw.net domain name for registration: "Virtual Works chose vw.net over other domain names not just because 'vw' reflected the company's own initials, but also because it foresaw the ability to profit from the natural association of vw.net and the VW mark." The court also found additional evidence of bad faith in Virtual Work's threat to auction the site to the highest bidder if Volkswagen did not elect to purchase it. "Virtual Works knew, both when it registered vw.net and when it offered to sell the site, that consumers would associate vw.net with Volkswagen. It sought to maximize the advantage of this association by threatening to auction off the site."

The ICANN uniform dispute resolution policy

On October 24, 1999, the Internet Corporation of Assigned Names and Numbers adopted a Uniform Dispute Resolution Policy (UDRP), which provides an alternative forum for resolving domain name disputes. All of the registrars for the .com, .net, and .org top-level domains adhere to the UDRP. The UDRP provides a system under which domain name registrants must submit disputes involving "abusive registrations" [40] to mandatory arbitration conducted by approved dispute resolution providers [41].

A complainant under paragraph 4(a) of the UDRP must prove that: (1) the respondent's domain name is "identical or confusingly similar to a trademark or service mark in which the complainant has rights"; (2) the respondent has "no rights or legitimate interests in respect of the domain name"; and (3) the respondent has shown bad faith in his registration and use of the domain name [42]. The first element of proof is usually easy to prove since it is the fact that led the complainant to challenge the respondent's domain name registration.

As to the second element, registrants may show that they have rights to or legitimate interests in a domain name by proving that even before they had any knowledge of the dispute, they were using or preparing to use the domain name "in connection with a bona fide offering of goods or services" [43] For instance, in *20th Century Fox Film Corp. v. Risser* [44], the registrant stated that he registered the domain name foxnetworknews.com, and other domain names that include the word "fox," to use for his proposed Web site design business. However, the panel rejected this as proof of legitimate interest since the proposed use had no rational relationship to the registered domain names. Likewise, speculation in hypothetical domain names has been rejected as proof of any right or legitimate interest, as in *Boardwalk Bank v. Thorogood* [45], where the respondent had registered 75 domain names, including boardwalkbank.com, but had not used any of them.

Registration of a domain name for the primary purpose of selling, renting, or otherwise transferring the name to the trademark owner is evidence of bad faith, the third element. For example, the panel found bad faith registration and use in *Julia Fiona Roberts v. Russell Boyd* [46] because the respondent registered juliaroberts.com and other domain names of famous movie and sports stars. This demonstrated bad faith, along with the fact that the respondent put the domain name up for on-line auction at eBay.com.

The primary advantage of the ICANN process is that it is often less cumbersome and lengthy than a lawsuit in court. A business that plans to register a domain name with an ICANN registrar should be sure to read and understand the dispute resolution procedure found in its registration agreement in case an issue like those described in this section arises.

Strategies for protecting trademarks on-line and avoiding disputes

The creator or owner of a Web site who wishes to use hyperlinks, frames, and metatags should avoid improperly using another's trademark or seek the written permission of the owner when a link, frame, or metatag contains trademarked logos and other material. Those seeking to use deep hyperlinks, frames, and metatags that contain trademarked logos and other material should first request written permission of the mark's owner. At the very least, the Web site owner should ensure that the original source is clearly visible. Additionally, Web pages containing hyperlinks and frames can be designed to clearly indicate that materials from another business are being retrieved and displayed.

As the facts leading to the *Ticketmaster* case suggest, it may be wise to seek authorization using a hyperlink licensing agreement before linking to a page located deep within a Web site. The agreement would probably not be necessary when linking to the site's home page or first page. Indeed, if a court were to classify all unauthorized linking as improper, the nature of the Internet would be severely undermined.

Another less elaborate protective measure is to post a disclaimer. It would state that the Web site and its owner are not sponsored by or affiliated with the owners of any trademarks used on the Web site, including any contained in the hyperlinks. In addition, the outcome in the *Total-News* case advises that those seeking to frame content from another Web site should first seek permission. Alternatively, a hyperlink could be used that connects directly to the provider's site or that opens a separate window to the provider's site. At the very least, it is probably wise for a business not to display content from another source in a frame that could be construed as misrepresenting the information as its own. Businesses should also avoid failing to acknowledge the actual source of information included on its Web site. It is possible to create dynamic Web pages that automatically alter their own URLs from time to time, making it difficult to maintain a frame or deep hyperlink to those pages. Javascript may also be employed to circumvent framing [47]. Likewise, it is possible to insert an instruction in a Web page's source code that opens the page in a new window separate from that of the framing page.

As a matter of standard practice, a business that owns a trademark should periodically use an Internet search engine, to perform a search using its trademark as a search term [48]. Doing this may reveal a hyperlink or frame. If the mark does not visually appear on a Web site, the HTML version of those sites can be viewed. This can be accomplished by using the browser's view source or document source features to determine if the mark is included as a metatag. If there is an unauthorized use of a trademark, the business should immediately investigate. The owner of the potentially infringing Web site should be notified that the site must either cease using or displaying the trademarked material, or negotiate for permission to use it.

Regarding domain names, a business that is planning to create an Internet presence should register its trademark as a domain name with a registry such as InterNIC. In doing so, the business should attempt to discover, by conducting a comprehensive trademark search, if any other business or person is currently using a potentially infringing or diluting domain name. If the business' intended market extends beyond the United States, the search should be international in scope. Domain names may be searched, for instance, through InterNIC's site located at rs.internic.net/rs-internic.html. In addition, it is easy to search for federally registered trademarks at the USPTO site at www.uspto.gov so as to avoid selecting another's trademark as a domain name. If so, the business should notify the domain name registrar of this and demand that the alleged infringer or diluter immediately cease using the name. Of course, if a business is creating an Internet presence and a domain name, it is best to not use another's registered trademark in the domain name in the first place. Doing a search through InterNIC's site can determine if this is a potential problem that may lead to a dilution or infringement claim. If there is a risk of doing so, the business should choose a product- or service-specific domain name to avoid such a claim. Thus, using unitedvanlines.com rather than united.com may avoid a potential legal dispute.

To more fully protect its domain name, however, a business should consider registering its domain name with the USPTO in order to gain an exclusive right of use. The USPTO will register a domain name as a trademark, so long as it is actually used as a trademark and not solely as an Internet address. Mere use as an Internet address will not meet the requirement that the mark be distinctive. The USPTO has issued an official policy statement on the use and registration of domain names as trademarks, which can be found at its site located at www.uspto.gov/web/uspto/info/domain.html. It is important that the domain name not be used merely as an address, however. The domain name should be displayed conspicuously on the Web site and in other advertising. In addition, registration creates a presumption of validity, ownership, and the right to use the mark. It also allows the owner to prevent importation into the country of goods that may infringe the mark, and allows the owner to seek an injunction against an alleged infringer.

In sum, trademark rights are a key asset of any business, and as we have seen, they have played a critical role in the development of e-commerce. It is not easy to say whether it has been trademark law that has most shaped business practices on the Internet, or whether it was the Internet that has been most responsible for changing trademark law in recent years. Either way, it is certain that trademarks will continue to be a key focus of both business and law on the Internet.

Notes

[1] 15 U.S.C. § 1127.

[2] Dueker, K., "Trademark Law Lost in Cyberspace: Trademark Protection for Internet Addresses," *Harvard Journal of Law & Technology*, Vol. 9, pp. 483.

[3] For instance, in *America Online, Inc. v. AT&T Corp.*, 1999 U.S Dist. Lexis 12615 (E.D. Va. 1999), the court held that plaintiff America Online, Inc.'s trade and service marks "You Have Mail," "IM," and "Buddy List" are generic and accordingly not entitled to trademark protection. As a result, the court determined that AT&T could continue to use these marks over AOL's objection in the operation of a competing service. The court reached this conclusion as a result of its application of the "primary significance test." "Under this test, a plaintiff who is seeking to establish a

valid trademark must show 'that the primary significance of the term in the minds of the consuming public is not the product but the producer.'" Applying this test, and analyzing the use to which AOL, its competitors, the trade and the media put the challenged marks, the court concluded that they were used for its ordinary meaning to describe the product itself, and not its producer. As such, the marks were generic and not entitled to protection under the Lanham Act.

[4] 15 U.S.C. § 1114.

[5] 839 F. Supp. 1552 (M.D. Fla. 1993).

[6] *Id.* at 1561.

[7] The Lanham Act also provides trademark owners a claim for unfair competition, which occurs when another creates confusion or a likelihood of confusion between the products or services as to source, sponsorship, or association. 15 U.S.C. § 1125(a).

[8] 15 U.S.C. § 1125.

[9] 15 U.S.C. §1127.

[10] No. 97-3055 DDP (C.D. Cal., filed April 28, 1997).

[11] *Ibid.*

[12] A thorough discussion of the legal issues posed by hyperlinking can be found in Jackson, M., "Linking Copyright to Homepages," *Fed. Comm. L.J.* Vol. 49, 1997, p. 731. Additional information about hyperlinking disputes can be found at Stefan Bechtold's "The Link Controversy Page" at www.jura.uni-tuebingen.de/~s-bes1/lcp.html.

[13] No. 97-1190 (S.D.N.Y. 1997).

[14] 45 U.S.P.Q. 2d (BNA) 2005 (C.D. Cal. 1998).

[15] No. 97-3204 CAL (N.D. Cal., filed August 1997).

[16] *Id.* at 1220, 1221. For other cases in which this practice was the subject of litigation, see *Playboy Enterprises, Inc. v. Asiafocus International, Inc.*, 1998 U.S. Dist. LEXIS 10359 (E.D. N.Y. 1998) (default judgment for plaintiffs in case asserting that the plaintiff's trademarks were infringed and diluted by blurring when the defendant embedded the plaintiff's trademarks in their Web site HTML code); *Insituform Technologies Inc. v. National Envirotech Group*, L.L.C., Civ No. 97-2064 (E.D. La. 1997) (consent judgment where defendant agreed to remove the plaintiff's trademarked slogans and graphical images from its Web site metatags); *Nilton Corp. v. Radiation Monitoring Devices, Inc.*, 27 F. Supp. 2d 102 (D. Mass. 1998) (enjoining the defendant's copying of Nilton's Web site metatags and HTML code); *Oppedahl & Larson v. Advanced Concepts*, No. 97cv1592 (D. Colo. 1997) (an action for trademark infringement for using metatags to divert traffic

to another site that has since settled out of court following the issuance of a permanent injunction). For a resource that collects information and links on metatag cases, see Meta Tag Lawsuits (visited May 1, 1998), http://searchenginewatch.com/resources/metasuits.html.

[17] 7 F. Supp. 2d 1098 (S.D. Cal. 1998).

[18] The defense to infringement is: "That the use of the name, term, or device charged to be an infringement is a use, otherwise than as a mark, of the party's individual name in his own business, or of the individual name of anyone in privity with such party, or of a term or device which is descriptive of and used fairly and in good faith only to describe the goods or services of such party, or their geographic origin...." 15 U.S.C. § 1115(b)(4).

[19] *Nihon Keizai Shimbun, Inc. v. Comline Business Data, Inc.*, 166 F. 3d 65, 73 (2d Cir. 1999) (citation omitted).

[20] The following shall not be actionable under this section: "(a) Fair use of a famous mark by another person in comparative commercial advertising or promotion to identify the competing goods or services of the owner of the famous mark. (b) Noncommercial use of a mark. (c) All forms of news reporting and news commentary." 15 U.S.C. § 1125(c)(4).

[21] *Id.* at 16–17 (citation omitted).

[22] *Id.* at 17.

[23] 1999 U.S. App. LEXIS 7779 (9th Cir. 1999).

[24] *Id.* at 77–78.

[25] *Id.* at 84.

[26] 55 F. Supp.2d 1070 (C.D. Cal. 1999), *aff'd* 202 F.3d 278 (9th Cir. 1999). See also *Estee Lauder, Inc. v. The Fragrance Counter, Inc.*, 189 F.R.D. 269 (1999).

[27] 55 F. Supp.2d 1070, 1085 (C.D. Cal. 1999).

[28] Baum, R., and R. Cumbow, "First Use: Key Test in Internet Domain Disputes," *National Law Journal*, February 12, 1996, p. C17.

[29] Burk, D., "Trademarks along the Infobahn: A First Look at the Emerging Law of Cybermarks," *Richmond Journal of Law and Technology*, Vol. 1, 1995, p. 1.

[30] Quittner, J., "Billions Registered: Right Now, There Are No Rules to Keep You from Owning a Bitchin' Corporate Name as Your Own Internet Address," *Wired*, October 1994, p. 50.

[31] 1996 U.S. Dist. LEXIS 14878 (N.D. Ill. 1996).

[32] *Id.*

[33] *Id.*

[34] *Id.* (citing *Panavision International v. Toeppen*, 945 F. Supp. 1296, 1303 (C.D. Cal. 1996). ("Registration of a trademark as a domain name, without more, is not a commercial use of the trademark and therefore is not within the prohibitions of the Act.")

[35] 15 U.S.C. § 1125(d)(1)(A).

[36] 15 U.S.C. § 1125(d)(1)(C).

[37] Nos. 98-7452 (L) , 98-7538 (XAP)(2d Cir. Feb. 2, 2000).

[38] *Id.*

[39] — F.3d — (4th Cir. 2001).

[40] Abusive registrations are those made with bad faith intent to profit commercially for others' trademarks, such as "cybersquatting" and "cyberpiracy."

[41] ICANN has approved four dispute resolution providers to implement the UDRP. They are the World Intellectual Property Organization (WIPO), the National Arbitration Forum (NAF), eResolution (DeC), and the CPR Institute.

[42] ICANN Uniform Domain Name Dispute Resolution Policy, par. 4(a), http://www.icann.org/udrp/udrp-policy-224oct99.htm.

[43] *Id.* par. 4(c)(i).

[44] NAF Case FA0093761 (decided Feb. 15, 2000).

[45] WIPO Case D2000-0213 (decided May 20, 2000).

[46] WIPO Case D2000-0210 (decided May 29, 2000).

[47] See Web Design Group, "Frames FAQ: Avoiding Getting Framed," (visited May 5, 1999) http://www.htmlhelp.com/design/frames/faq/framed.html; http://www.wired.com/news/technology/story/2844.html; SiteShield http://www.maximized.com.

[48] Not surprisingly, there are now on-line services—such as MarkWatch (www.markwatch.com), NetSearchers (www.netsearchers.com.uk), Thomson & Thomson (www.namestake.com), and MicroPatent (www.marksearch.com)—that will monitor trademarks on the Internet.

6

On-line copyright protection and infringement

The United States Constitution grants Congress the power to protect authors by giving them certain exclusive rights in their works. The rapid transmission of data and information facilitated by the Internet is both a blessing and a threat to an author's exclusive rights. Indeed, few areas of law have been so heavily litigated in the digital age as has copyright law. Like trademarks, a copyright is a form of intangible or "intellectual" property that is protected under federal law. Whether a business is engaged in writing software, servicing and repairing computers, maintaining a Web site or a network, or transmitting material electronically, the business should be concerned with its rights and potential liabilities under copyright law. This chapter examines the scope of copyright protection in the on-line setting, and suggests measures to protect a copyright in a digital work and to avoid liability for the infringement of another's work.

Basic requirements for copyright protection

The Copyright Act grants exclusive rights to authors of certain types of creative works, whether published or unpublished. To be protected under the Copyright Act, these must be "*original* works of authorship *fixed* in any tangible medium of *expression* from which they can be perceived, reproduced, or otherwise communicated either directly or with the aid of a machine or device" [1]. Over the years, the courts have interpreted the basic requirements of the act, and applied them to a range of creations.

Works of authorship

The Copyright Act extends to sound recordings as well as literary, dramatic, musical, choreographic, architectural, pictorial, and sculptural works. Computer programs and most database compilations may be registered as "literary works" if they meet the other requirements for protection. The courts have also instructed that copyright protects the way that an idea is expressed, and not the idea itself. Thus, procedures, methods of operation, systems, processes, concepts, principles, discoveries, or devices, as distinguished from a description, explanation, or illustration, are not copyrightable [2]. Likewise, titles and names, short phrases and slogans, familiar symbols or designs, mere listings of ingredients or contents, and basic variations of typographic ornamentation, lettering, or coloring are not eligible for copyright protection.

Computer programs and software are considered to be copyrightable literary works under the Copyright Act. A 1980 amendment to the Copyright Act defined a computer program as "a set of statements or instructions to be used directly or indirectly in a computer in order to bring about a certain result" [3]. In numerous cases since 1980, the courts have held that software is protectable expression written in the language of computer code. In the leading case of *Apple Computer, Inc. v. Franklin Computer Corp.* [4], the court determined that it makes no difference to the issue of protectability whether the program is expressed in source code or object code, or embodied on read only memory or in an operating system.

The copyrightability of the nonliteral aspects of software has proven to be a closer question for the courts. In *Lotus Development Corp. v. Borland International, Inc.* [5], a decision affirmed in 1996 by an equally divided United States Supreme Court, a federal court of appeals held that a spreadsheet program's menu command hierarchy was not copyrightable because it was essentially more of a method of operating the program rather than a form of expression. As to whether the "look and feel" of a computer program is protected, the court in the leading case of *Computer Associates International, Inc. v. Altai, Inc.* [6], held that a screen display, or graphical user interface, is not copyrightable to the extent that it is a functional or utilitarian aspect of the program's structure and not a form of protectable expression.

Originality requirement

The courts have held that the originality requirement is quite low and requires only that the work demonstrate some minimal level of creativity and not be substantially similar to another's work. This standard does not require novelty or uniqueness, but only that the work not have been copied from another. An audiovisual screen display of a program is considered original if, when examined as a whole, its component images have been combined in some creative sequence [7].

The element of originality has been of central concern in determining whether computer databases and similar compilations are protectable by copyright. In *Feist Publications, Inc. v. Rural Telephone Service Co., Inc.* [8], the United States Supreme Court considered the extent of copyright protection for a telephone directory and concluded that while each of the individual data is not protected, because they are facts and material in the public domain, the selection, arrangement, and coordination of the data can be protected if done in a sufficiently creative or original way. Although the collection and compilation of electronic data often involves great time and effort, this standard means that the resulting database will not be eligible for copyright protection unless the process for selecting the data and the resulting arrangement demonstrated some degree of originality [9].

This standard has been applied in two recent cases involving the West Publishing Company's compilations of judicial opinions and other legal materials. In one case, the court held that HyperLaw, Inc., a company that publishes CD-ROM compilations of federal court cases, was entitled to copy information specifying the names of the parties and their attorneys, courts, dates of decision, alternative citations, and case history that West had compiled because they lacked even minimal creativity [10]. In another case, the same court held that West's page numbering and cross-referencing system for its WESTLAW computer database was also not sufficiently creative to warrant copyright protection [11]. However, another court reached the opposite conclusion in an earlier case, holding that the pagination was part of West's original arrangement of the cases and that the publisher of the LEXIS computer legal research service had infringed West's copyright by inserting West's page numbers in its database [12]. In contrast to the approach of the courts in the United States, the European Union implemented a directive in 1996 to provide a special 15-year-long form of protection to the contents of databases and to prevent the reuse of those contents for commercial purposes.

Fixation requirement

The requirement of fixation is met when the work is embodied in a tangible copy or phonorecord and "is sufficiently permanent or stable to permit it to be perceived, reproduced, or otherwise communicated for" longer than a merely transitory period of time. By contrast, extemporaneous speeches, improvisational musical or theatrical performances, and choreographic works that have not been written, notated, or recorded are not fixed.

In the context of computer technology, the fixation requirement has not been a fiercely debated issue. In the case of *Midway Manufacturing Co. v. Artic International, Inc.* [13], for instance, the court found that the audiovisual displays of an electronic game were fixed and reproducible even though images changed rapidly. Similarly, in *MAI Systems Corp. v. Peak Computer, Inc.* [14], the court decided that the loading of software into RAM memory constituted fixation whenever the program was run.

Copyright ownership and duration

Copyright protection extends to all published and unpublished works, regardless of the nationality or domicile of the author. The copyright vests at the time the work is created in fixed form and immediately becomes the property of the author who created the work. No publication or registration with the Copyright Office is required to obtain a copyright. In addition, the use of a copyright notice © is no longer required under U.S. law [15], although it is often advisable because it informs the public that the work is protected by copyright, identifies the copyright owner, and shows the year of the first publication. If the work is infringed, and a proper notice of copyright appears on the published copy to which the defendant had access, then the defendant cannot argue that he or she did not realize that the work was protected and thereby reduce the amount of damages for which he or she may be liable.

Ownership of works for hire and joint works

Only the author, or those who have been given a license or been assigned the copyright by the author, can rightfully enforce the copyright. On occasion, the copyright does not vest in the original author because he or she was hired as an employee to create the work. When a work has been made for hire, the employer and not the employee is considered to be the author. The Copyright Act defines a "work made for hire" as:

> (1) a work prepared by an employee within the scope of his or her employment; or
>
> (2) a work specially ordered or commissioned for use as a contribution to a collective work, as a part of a motion picture or other audiovisual work, as a translation, as a supplementary work, as a compilation, as an instructional text, as a test, as answer material for a test, or as an atlas, if the parties expressly agree in a written instrument signed by them that the work shall be considered a work made for hire....

The authors of a joint work, such a periodical or collection, are co-owners of the copyright in the work, unless there is an agreement to the contrary. However, the copyright in each separate contribution to a periodical or other collective work is distinct from copyright in the collective work as a whole and vests initially with the author of the contributed work.

Transfer of copyright

Copyright owners are free to transfer by contract or will any or all of their exclusive rights to one or multiple persons. The rights are infinitely divisible, so that the author of a book can transfer the right to make copies of the book to A, the right to sell and distribute the copies to B, and the right to make a theatrical adaptation to C. The transfer may be exclusive to one person, or nonexclusive so that multiple persons could make copies, sell, or adapt the book. A transfer of exclusive rights must be in writing and signed by the copyright owner, whereas transfer of a right on a nonexclusive basis does not require a written agreement [16]. The mere transfer of ownership of a book, manuscript, painting, or any other copy or phonorecord does not transfer the copyright to the possessor.

Copyright term

A work originally created on or after January 1, 1978, has a term of copyright protection lasting for the author's life plus an additional 70 years after his or her death. In the case of "a joint work prepared by two or more authors who did not work for hire," the term lasts for 70 years after the last surviving author's death. For works made for hire, the duration of the copyright is 95 years from publication or 120 years from creation, whichever is shorter. Under the copyright law in effect before 1978, copyright vested either on the date a work was published with a copyright notice, or on the date of registration if the work was registered in unpublished form. The copyright received a first term of 28 years from the date it was obtained. In the final (28th) year of the first term, the copyright was eligible for renewal for another 28-year term. The current Copyright Act extended the renewal term from 28 to 67 years, with a total term of protection of 95 years.

Exclusive rights of copyright owners

The Copyright Act provides copyright owners with several exclusive rights. The author has the sole right to do or authorize others to do any or all of the following [17]:

- To reproduce the work in the form of copies or phonorecords;
- To prepare adaptations or "derivative works" based upon the original work;
- To distribute copies or phonorecords of the work to the public by sale, or by rental, lease, or lending;
- To perform the work publicly, in the case of literary, musical, dramatic, and choreographic works, pantomimes, and motion pictures and other audiovisual works;
- To display the copyrighted work publicly, in the case of literary, musical, dramatic, and choreographic works, pantomimes, and pictorial, graphic, or sculptural works, including the individual images of a motion picture or other audiovisual work; and in the case of sound recordings, to perform the work publicly by means of a digital audio transmission.

Copyright infringement and Internet issues

When anyone other than the copyright owner or the lawful transferee of a copyright exercises any of the exclusive rights afforded by the Copyright Act, there is an infringement of the copyright and the owner may sue for damages. Infringement need not be intentional and may be done subconsciously or innocently. Moreover, the plaintiff need not prove that he or she suffered any actual damages as a result of the infringement. Instead, the plaintiff must prove that he or she is the owner of a valid copyright, that the defendant copied or used the work, and that the copying or use was done without permission.

Proving impermissible copying or use requires that the plaintiff demonstrate that the defendant had access to the work and there is substantial similarity between the plaintiff's original work and defendant's allegedly infringing work. To prove access, the plaintiff must demonstrate that the defendant had some reasonable opportunity to view or come into contact with the plaintiff's work, though access may be presumed if the work is widely distributed. To prove substantial similarity between the works, the plaintiff need not show verbatim, identical copying. Rather, the courts have developed several standards for evaluating the degree of congruence between the two works based on attributes of the works. Some courts look to see whether the basic, overall pattern or structure of the original work is reproduced in the allegedly infringing work. Other courts apply a process that attempts to define the levels of abstraction in the work from the general idea behind the work to the specific details of the expression, and then compares the similarities between the specific details in each of the works to determine the degree of identity between them.

The Internet has proven to be a particularly fertile ground for copyright infringement issues. Most frequently, the courts have encountered claims of infringement involving a copyright owner's exclusive rights to reproduce, distribute, make derivative works, and publicly display or perform his or her works on-line. In various cases, the courts have determined that the displaying of unauthorized copies of electronic clip art, texts, graphic and music files, and photographs on Web pages violated the copyright owner's rights of reproduction and public display, performance, and distribution [18].

Of particular note regarding on-line infringement is the question of whether the use of hyperlinks and frames may lead to liability. A hyperlink connects a user to another Web site when the user clicks on the highlighted text or graphic image. Deep linking occurs when a hyperlink bypasses another Web site's home page and connects the user directly to an internal page. For instance, instead of linking to the home page of an on-line publication, a deep link might take the user directly to an article within the publication's Web site.

Although it is not infringement merely to create a hyperlink, it is a violation of the law to create a link that contributes to unauthorized copying of a copyrighted work if the linking party knew or had reason to know of the unauthorized copying and encouraged it. In *Intellectual Reserve, Inc. v. Utah Lighthouse Ministry, Inc.* [19], for instance, the defendant posted infringing copies of a church's copyrighted handbook at its Web site. The Web site was ordered to remove the handbook, but subsequently provided links to other sites that contained infringing copies of the handbook. The court found that these links were infringing because they were different from traditional hyperlinks because the Web site knew and encouraged the use of the links to obtain unauthorized copies.

As to the deep linking, however, another court has ruled that the use of deep links did not amount to copyright infringement and analogized the technique to using a library's card index to get referrals to particular items. In the *Ticketmaster Corp. v. Tickets.com* [20] case, Tickets.com, an on-line ticket service, provided deep links to Ticketmaster Web pages to provide users with certain ticket purchases. Tickets.com had prefaced the link by stating "These tickets are sold by another ticketing company. Although we can't sell them to you, the link above will take you directly to the other company's website where you can purchase them."

Framing has also led to several infringement suits on the theory that the framing site alters the appearance of the framed site's content. Framing is a technique that allows a user at one Web site to view the contents of another Web site within a frame without leaving the first Web site. In the case of *Futuredontics, Inc. v. Applied Anagramic, Inc.* [21], the defendant Web site owner had framed the content from the Web site of a competitor. The frames included the competitor's trademark and links to all of its Web pages. The court ruled that a Web site containing a link that reproduced the plaintiff's Web pages within a frame may constitute infringement, reasoning that the addition of the frame modified the appearance of the linked site and such modifications could, without authorization, amount to a derivative work and an infringement of the plaintiff's exclusive adaptation right.

Contributory and vicarious infringement

As distinguished from direct infringement, where the defendant is the primary violator of a copyright owner's exclusive rights, contributory infringement occurs when the defendant knows of and participates in the infringing activities of another. Vicarious liability for infringement results when the defendant controls or supervises another, such as an agent, and receives a financial benefit from the other's infringing activities.

Claims based on these types of indirect infringement on the Internet have arisen in the context of electronic bulletin boards. In *Sega Enterprises Ltd. v. Maphia* [22], for example, the defendant operated a bulletin board that contained and distributed unauthorized copies of Sega copyrighted video game software. Sega sued for contributory and vicarious infringement when it discovered that users of the bulletin board were allowed to upload and download the games. The court found that the defendant knew that his users were copying the games and had provided the facility to do so with the expectation of profit. As such, the court concluded that the defendant was liable for contributory infringement of Sega's copyright.

Similarly, in *Playboy Enterprises, Inc. v. Webbworld, Inc.* [23], the defendant operated a Web site containing unauthorized copies of images acquired through use of its program, which automatically scanned Usenet newsgroups for images that had been posted without permission, downloaded and reformatted them, and allowed subscribers to download them for a fee. Wnen Playboy discovered that its copyrighted photographs were being reproduced and distributed on this site, it sued for infringement. Among other conclusions, the court held that the defendant was vicariously liable because he had created the scanning program and supervised the Web site, even though he had not originally uploaded the infringing images to Usenet.

Fair use as a defense

While it is unlawful for anyone to violate any of the rights provided by the Copyright Act to the owner of copyright, these rights are not unlimited in scope. The Copyright Act establishes limitations on these rights. In some cases, these limitations are specified exemptions from copyright liability. One major limitation is the doctrine of fair use. Fair use limits the exclusive rights of the copyright owner and serves as a defense to a claim of infringement. The defense applies to use of the copyrighted work for purposes of criticism, comment, news reporting, teaching, scholarship, and research.

In assessing whether the fair use doctrine applies, the courts will consider the:

- *Purpose and character of the use:* whether the original work was used without permission for commercial purposes or for nonprofit educational purposes. A for-profit use argues against fair use, though use for nonprofit and educational reasons must be limited.
- *Nature of the copyrighted work:* whether the work is factual or informational, or creative or imaginative. The more factual, newsworthy, or informative the original work, the more probable that the use was fair.
- *Amount and substantiality of the amount of the original work used in relation to the whole work:* whether the percentage of the work taken was significant. Even if the quantity of the amount taken is small, it is considered substantial if it represents the core or key point of the work as a whole.
- *Effect on the market or value of the original work:* whether and to what degree the defendant's use of the work undermines the owner's incentive for creating the work and the commercial market for the work or its derivative works.

The defense of fair use was considered in *Los Angeles Times, Inc. v. Free Republic* [24], in which the defendant was the operator of an electronic bulletin board service. The entire text of articles published on the *Los Angeles Times'* Web sites was posted on the defendant's Web site so that its members could add their own opinions and commentary. The newspaper sued, alleging that the unauthorized copying and posting of its articles on the Web site constituted copyright infringement. The defendant invoked the fair use doctrine, arguing that it was necessary to copy, verbatim, the newspaper's articles to allow Web site users to criticize the manner in which the media covered current events.

In balancing the fair use factors, the court reasoned that the newspaper had demonstrated that the availability of verbatim copies on the defendant's Web site potentially interfered with its attempts to exploit the market for viewing the articles on-line, for selling copies of archived articles, and for licensing others to display or sell the articles. Because the copying was verbatim, encompassed large numbers of articles, and occurred on an almost daily basis, evidence supported findings that the defendant engaged in extensive, systematic copying of the newspaper's protected works. Although the character of the defendant's Web site was noncommercial, the defendant did not demonstrate that verbatim copying of the articles was necessary to achieve its critical purpose. As such, the court rejected the fair use argument.

Digital Millennium Copyright Act

The Congress amended the Copyright Act in 1998 by the Digital Millennium Copyright Act (DMCA) [25], which contains several provisions of importance to on-line businesses. The DMCA prohibits circumvention of any technological measures that restrict access to a copyrighted work, such as password protection or encryption. For instance, circumvention would occur if a file containing an encrypted copyrighted work was decrypted, or if a password protection device was deactivated or bypassed to gain access to a copyrighted work. Producing or importing such circumvention products or services is also prohibited. The DMCA also prohibits removal or alteration of copyright management information from a copyrighted work. Copyright management information includes copyright notices, names of authors or owners of the work, terms or conditions for use of the work, and numbers or symbols that link to this information.

Additionally, the DMCA limits the liability of ISPs for: copyright infringement resulting from the passive transmission of infringing material between users; temporary or intermediate storage or caching of infringing material on their networks or servers by users; and for hyperlinking to Web sites containing infringing material. The DMCA narrowly defines an Internet service provider as a business that offers "transmission, routing, or...connections for digital on-line communications, between or among points specified by a user of material of the user's choosing, without modification of the material." To receive protection from liability under the DMCA, ISPs must adopt and inform Internet users of a policy for terminating service in response to repeated incidents of infringing activity and ensure standard technical measures used by copyright owners to identify or protect their works on-line.

Finally, the DMCA allows the owner of a computer to make a copy of a program during repair or maintenance of the computer. Thus, the DMCA overruled the decision in *MAI Systems Corp. v. Peak Computer, Inc.*, discussed above, where the court held that a computer maintenance and repair service was liable for copyright infringement when it made copies of a copyrighted program in RAM, while loading and running the software during its repairs. To be eligible for this exemption from liability, the copying must result solely by activating a computer loaded with a lawfully acquired copy of the program, and must occur during the authorized repair or maintenance of the computer, and be destroyed immediately after those repairs or maintenance are completed.

In two cases of note, the courts have interpreted the various "safe harbor" provisions of the DMCA. The case of *Kelly v. Arriba Soft Corp.* [26], involved the interplay of the DMCA and the fair use doctrine. The defendant, Ditto, operated a "visual search engine" that retrieved, through use of an Internet crawler, graphical images in response to a search query entered by the user. Unlike other search engines, however, the defendant produced a list of reduced, thumbnail pictures related to the user's query. By clicking on the desired thumbnail, a user could view the image attributes window displaying the full-size version of the image, a description of its dimensions, and an address for the Web site where it originated. By clicking on the address, the user could link to the originating Web site for the image.

The plaintiff, a photographer who had published several books, sued for copyright infringement when she discovered that 35 of her images were indexed by the search engine and put in the defendant's image database. As a result, these images were made available in thumbnail form to users of the defendant's visual search engine. She also argued that the defendant violated the DMCA by displaying thumbnails of her images without displaying the corresponding copyright management information consisting of standard copyright notices in the surrounding text. The defendant relied on fair use as a defense.

As to the DMCA claim, the court found no violation because the copyright management information remained available to users:

> There is no dispute the [search engine] removed Plaintiff's images from the context of Plaintiff's Web sites where their copyright management information was located, and converted them to thumbnails in Defendant's index. There is also no dispute the Arriba Vista search engine allowed full-size images to be viewed without their copyright management information. Defendant's users could obtain a full-sized version of a thumb-

> nailed image by clicking on the thumbnail. A user who did this was given the name of the Web site from which Defendant obtained the image, where any associated copyright management information would be available, and an opportunity to link there. Users were also informed on Defendant's Web site that use restrictions and copyright limitations may apply to images retrieved by Defendant's search engine.

As to whether fair use was a defense to the copyright infringement claim, the court found that two of the four fair use factors weighed in favor of fair use, and two weighed against it. The first and fourth factors (character of use and lack of market harm) weighed in favor of a fair use finding because of the established importance of search engines and the "transformative" nature of using reduced versions of images to organize and provide access to them. The second and third factors (creative nature of the work and amount or substantiality of copying) weigh against fair use. However, the court reasoned that the first factor of the fair use test is the most important in this case:

> Defendant never held Plaintiff's work out as its own, or even engaged in conduct specifically directed at Plaintiff's work. Plaintiff's images were swept up along with two million others available on the Internet, as part of Defendant's efforts to provide its users with a better way to find images on the Internet. Defendant's purposes were and are inherently transformative, even if its realization of those purposes was at times imperfect. Where, as here, a new use and new technology are evolving, the broad transformative purpose of the use weighs more heavily than the inevitable flaws in its early stages of development.... The Court finds Defendant's conduct constituted fair use of Plaintiff's images.

The defendant in the case of *A&M Records, Inc. v. Napster* [27] did not fare as well. Napster was a popular Internet site that facilitated subscribers' sharing of digital music MP3 files, many of which were protected by copyright. Napster provided its subscribers with a search engine to locate MP3 files on the Internet and a tool for retrieving and playing the desired files. The recording industry brought suit for infringement and Napster claimed immunity under the DMCA, which limits liability "for infringement [committed by its users] by reason of the [service] provider's transmitting, routing, or providing connections for, material through a system or network controlled or operated by or for the service provider, or by reason of the intermediate and transient storage of that material in the course of such transmitting, routing, or providing connections."

The district court, however, ruled that Napster could not make use of this safe harbor for two reasons. First, the court found that Napster "does not transmit, route or provide connections through its system" and therefore is not an ISP. Napster's role was not that of a passive conduit for information; rather, Napster provided the means to find and retrieve copyrightable material. Second, the court observed that the DMCA also requires an ISP to maintain a copyright compliance policy if it wants to take advantage of the safe harbor. Even if Napster were an ISP, the court concluded, its copyright compliance policy was not adequate. Further, the court found that Napster was not protected by the fair use defense.

The Ninth Circuit Court of Appeals later affirmed the district court's judgment. On appeal, Napster again argued that its users did not directly infringe the plaintiffs' copyrights because the users are engaged in a fair use of the material by sampling, by which users made temporary copies before purchasing; and "space shifting," by which users accessed sound recordings that they already owned using the Napster system. The court applied the fair use analysis and agreed with the district court that the Napster users were not making fair use of the recordings. Specifically, the appellate court found that the recordings were creative works and their wholesale copying by Napster users was commercial because many users got "something for free they would normally have to buy." Addressing Napster's effect on the plaintiffs' market, the court of appeals stated that Napster harmed the market in at least two ways: (1) it reduced audio CD sales among college students; and (2) it raised the barriers to the plaintiffs' entry into the market for the digital music downloading. As such, the fair use defense was not applicable.

The Ninth Circuit also affirmed the district court's finding that Napster's users had directly infringed the plaintiffs' copyrighted recordings and that Napster, because it knew of this, "materially contribute[d] to the infringement" and was therefore a contributory and vicarious infringer. Finally, the court affirmed the district court's determination that the DMCA did not immunize Napster from liability. As the *Napster* decision reveals, any firm adopting an on-line business model that involves distribution of copyrighted files, software, or other materials without express permission will be hard pressed to argue that any resulting infringement is excusable because of fair use or compliance with the DMCA.

Protecting copyright and avoiding infringement on-line

If a business is generating any type of copyrightable product or materials, it should consider registering the copyright with the U.S. Copyright Office [28]. Even though registration is not a requirement for protection, there are several advantages to doing so. Registration is inexpensive, establishes a public record of copyright ownership and, if made before or within five years of publication, registration will establish a presumption of validity of the copyright, making the burden of proof easier for the copyright owner suing for infringement. Indeed, before an infringement suit may be filed in court, registration is necessary for works of U.S. origin [29]. If registration is made within three months after publication of the work or prior to an infringement of the work, statutory damages and attorney's fees will be available to the copyright owner in court actions [30]. Otherwise, only an award of actual damages and profits is available [31].

The most obvious means to avoid liability for copyright infringement is to not copy or publicly display, distribute, or perform another's copyrighted material without authorization. Seeking permission in the form of a license agreement is much cheaper than the potential damages that can be awarded for infringement. When it comes to linking and framing, the easiest method of avoiding linking problems is to seek permission. Linking to material known to be infringing may result in liability, as was the case in the *Intellectual Reserve* case discussed earlier. It is probable that permission is not required for a hyperlink that uses a hyperlink to another Web site's homepage, but it makes sense to ask for permission through a written linking agreement for deep links and frames. Taking this precaution may avoid the type of claims raised in the *Ticketmaster* and *Futuredontics* cases discussed above. If another seeks permission to create a deep link or frame to your Web site, be sure to include terms and conditions of use. By spelling out terms and conditions of use, the Web site owner can control how and where the licensee can and cannot link to or frame content on the Web site [32]. To minimize liability for any infringing conduct on the other Web site, a business may want to include a prominently displayed linking disclaimer waiving liability for a potentially infringing materials or activities on other Web sites. While disclaimers are not a fool proof means for avoiding liability, they may mitigate damages.

Finally, an ISP should comply with the provisions of the DMCA [33]. Under the DMCA, an ISP can avoid liability for contributory or vicarious copyright infringement should one of its subscribers place an infringing copy on-line by following the "notice and takedown" provisions, which require that once an ISP receives notice of the infringement, it must take down the unauthorized material. In addition, the ISP must designate and register with a Copyright Office agent to receive notices from copyright owners, and must implement a policy of terminating the accounts of subscribers who are repeat infringers [34]. The U.S. Copyright Office Web site provides a wealth of information and forms that make it quite easy to register a copyright and comply with the Copyright Act and DMCA requirements [35].

As this chapter reveals, irrespective of whether a business develops and distributes software, has created an electronic database, or transacts business on-line through a carefully designed Web site, it has made a substantial capital investment that should be protected from unauthorized use and copying. If the software, database, or content meets the requirements for copyrightability, then the business has exclusive rights under federal law that allow it to earn potential licensing revenue and guard against infringement by others.

Endnotes

[1] 17 U.S.C. § 101.

[2] *Id.* § 102(b).

[3] *Id.*

[4] 714 F.2d 1240 (1983), *cert. denied*, 464 U.S. 1033 (1984).

[5] 49 F.3d 807 (1st Cir. 1995), *aff'd by an equally divided Court*, 516 U.S. 233 (1996).

[6] 982 F.2d 698 (2d Cir. 1992).

[7] *See Atari Games Corp. v. Oman*, 888 F.2d 878 (1989).

[8] 499 U.S. 340 (1991).

[9] *Accord CDN v. Kapes*, No. 98-55555 (9th Cir. 1999) (holding that a database of coin prices that had been used to create content for defendant's Web site was sufficiently original and protectable by copyright).

[10] *Matthew Bender & Co. and HyperLaw, Inc. v. West Publishing Co.*, 158 F.3d 674 (1998).

[11] *Matthew Bender & Co. and HyperLaw, Inc. v. West Publishing Co.*, 158 F.3d 693 (1998).

[12] 799 F.2d 1219 (8th Cir. 1986).

[13] 547 F. Supp. 999, *aff'd*, 704 F.2d 1009 (7th Cir. 1982).

[14] 991 F.2d 511 (9th Cir. 1993).

[15] See 17 U.S.C. §§ 401–406. Copyright notice was required under prior law, but the United States, as a signatory to the Berne Convention, a multinational treaty on copyright law, discontinued the notice requirement to comply with the treaty beginning in 1988.

[16] 17 U.S.C. §§ 204–205.

[17] In addition to the rights discussed in the main text, certain authors of works of visual art have the moral rights of attribution and integrity that ensure that their names are associated with their works and protect their works from mutilation and unauthorized modification.

[18] See *Michaels v. Internet Entertainment Group, Inc.*, 5 F. Supp. 2d 823 (C.D. Cal. 1998) (clip art); *Marobie-FL, Inc. v. National Ass'n of Fire Equipment.* Distributors, 983 F. Supp. 1167 (N.D. Ill. 1997) (clip art); *Playboy Enterprises, Inc. v. Frena*, 839 F. Supp. 1552 (M.D. Fla. 1993) (photographs).

[19] 75 F. Supp. 2d 1290 (D. Utah 1999).

[20] No. 99-7654 (C.D. Cal. 2000).

[21] 46 U.S.P.Q. 2d 2005 (C.D. Cal. 1997).

[22] 948 F. Supp. 923 (N.D. Cal. 1996).

[23] 968 F. Supp. 1171 (N.D. Tex. 1997).

[24] 2000 U.S. Dist. LEXIS 5669 (C.D. Cal. 2000).

[25] 17 U.S.C. § 1201 *et seq.*

[26] No. SA CV 99-560 GLT[JW] (C.D. Cal. 2000).

[27] 2001 WL 115033 (9th Cir. 2001).

[28] There is no form of international copyright protection available; thus, copyright registrations must be filed in each country in which the work may be used.

[29] 17 U.S.C. § 411.

[30] The plaintiff may sue for actual damages suffered, lost profits earned by the defendant due to the infringement, statutory damages of between $200 and $100,000 per work infringed depending upon whether the infringement was willfully or innocently done, attorney's fees, and injunctive relief. *Id.* § 412.

[31] *Id.*

[32] For a useful checklist of points to consider including in such an agreement, see Liberto, S. M., "A Checklist for Hyperlink Agreements," August 1998, www.libertolaw.com/articles.html.

[33] See Smith, M. F. and A. Bruggeman, "Internet and Web site Management Under the Digital Millennium Copyright Act," *The Licensing Journal*, Feb. 2000, p. 9 (detailing the procedures for complying with the DMCA).

[34] See *id.* § 512.

[35] United States Copyright Office, www.loc.gov/copyright/.

7

Electronic mail privacy in the workplace

Electronic mail, or e-mail, has emerged as one of the fastest and most popular communications tools. E-mail combines the spontaneous, informal nature of oral communication with the recorded, visual nature of written correspondence. In the workplace, the use of e-mail can enhance efficiency and creativity in ways that traditional written memoranda, letters, and reports cannot. Similarly, e-mail can easily be reduced to hard copy, allowing either the sender or recipient to memorialize their communication in a way not easily done with oral discussions or telephone conversations.

Of course, there is also a downside to the use and accessibility of e-mail in the business environment. Employees may use e-mail with little reflection for personal purposes or compose messages that contain content that is unprofessional or otherwise inappropriate for the workplace. Such communications may adversely implicate the legal rights of others, with consequences both to the employee and the employer. At the same time, many employees may assume incorrectly that their e-mail communications are always private and unrecorded.

E-mail and employee privacy

The ease with which we can use e-mail for personal communication sometimes means that we may give little in the way of second thought to how we might use it in the home workplace. Employees and employers often do not realize that e-mail messages do not disappear after deletion, but instead remain on hard drive until the trash directory is emptied, or are stored and retrievable on tape or on a server as backed-up copies. Even if the e-mail was sent through an Internet-based e-mail program, it may have passed through several servers and been stored as a copy on each one. As such, if the content of employee e-mail is inappropriate or unlawful, the employer may face potential liability pursuant to basic principles of agency law.

An agency relationship exists when one person (the agent) is authorized by another person (the principal) to act on behalf of and under the control of the principal. Under the doctrine of *respondeat superior*, which means "let the master answer," a principal-employer is liable for the unlawful acts of an agent-employee when he or she commits the acts within the scope of his or her employment. This rule is one of *vicarious* liability for the employer because the liability is premised on his or her relationship with the employee rather than on any fault on his or her part.

Thus, under the doctrine of respondeat superior, e-mail that contains sexual or racial content that creates a hostile work environment may lead to claims for unlawful harassment. E-mail containing false statements about other persons may result in a suit for defamation, and an employer may face criminal prosecution if an employee sends child pornography using employer e-mail. Additionally, an employer may be sued for infringement if an employee reproduces, distributes, or otherwise appropriates materials protected by copyright or trademark in e-mail transmissions.

The risks to an employer posed by an employee's on-line behavior are illustrated in the case of *Blakey v. Continental Airlines* [1]. Blakey, a female pilot, sued Continental for defamation, infliction of emotional distress, and hostile work environment sexual harassment stemming from comments that her fellow employees had posted on Continental's electronic bulletin board forum. She alleged that Continental failed to stop employees from exchanging sexually derogatory comments about her even after she complained. Continental argued that it should not be held liable for the alleged harassment because the harassing behavior by its employees did not take place within the workplace or at a place under its physical control. The New Jersey Supreme Court disagreed, holding that the electronic bulletin board forum was sufficiently integrated with Continental's operations so as to provide a benefit to the airline. Further, the court stated that employers are required to take effective measures to stop unlawful harassment when they know of it. Because Continental had notice of the harassing online conduct, and that the conduct complained of was severe or pervasive enough to make a reasonable person believe that the working environment was hostile, Continental had a duty to remedy the situation [2].

Moreover, the case of *Konop v. Hawaiian Airlines, Inc.* [3] illustrates the risks to the employer due to the actions of one of its managers. Konop, a pilot for Hawaiian Airlines, created a Web site on which he posted statements that were critical of his employer and its union. Konop's Web site was password-protected and Hawaiian Airlines managers and union officials were not allowed to gain access. Nonetheless, Hawaiian's vice president logged onto Konop's site using another employee's name and discovered statements accusing him of fraud and other misconduct. After Konop was warned that he might be sued for defamation, he discovered how the vice president had gained access to his site and sued Hawaiian for illegal wiretapping. The court held that accessing a password-protected Web site without authorization was unlawful and that Hawaiian Airlines was responsible for the vice president's actions.

Workplace monitoring and employee privacy

How then can an employer reduce its exposure to liability for the consequences of employee misuse of e-mail, but also avoid employee claims for invasion of privacy if the employer intercepts or monitors employee e-mail? The ambit of employee privacy rights in the private sector is quite limited. The Fourth Amendment to the United States Constitution, which requires probable cause as a prerequisite to searching files, desks, lockers, or offices, does not apply to private sector employees [4]. However, the Fourth Amendment protects public sector employees from unreasonable searches and seizures by government agents, including government employers or supervisors.

In *United States v. Simons*, an employee of the FBI was indicted on one count of knowingly receiving child pornography after a warrantless search of his computer revealed that he had a number of sexually explicit photos of minors stored on his hard drive. The employee, Simons, argued that the search unconstitutionally violated his legitimate expectation of privacy. The court, however, concluded that Simons' Fourth Amendment rights were not violated by the FBI's retrieval of Simons' hard drive from his office. According to the court, Simons did not have a legitimate expectation of privacy regarding his Internet use, in light of the FBI's Internet policy, which clearly stated that FBI would "audit, inspect, and/or monitor" employees' use of the Internet, including all file transfers, all Web sites visited, and all e-mail messages, "as deemed appropriate." This policy placed employees on notice that they could not reasonably expect that their Internet activity would be private. Accordingly, FBI's search and seizure of the computer files Simons downloaded from the Internet did not violate the Fourth Amendment.

The Electronic Communications Privacy Act (ECPA) is another potential source of privacy rights for employees. Under the ECPA,

> whoever (1) intentionally accesses without authorization a facility through which an electronic communication service is provided; or (2) intentionally exceeds an authorization to access that facility; and thereby obtains, alters, or prevents authorized access to a wire or electronic communication while it is in electronic storage in such system shall be punished [by fine or imprisonment as provided] [5].

A violation of the ECPA carries a fine up to $10,000 and one year of imprisonment. While on its face, this statute appears to limit the employer's ability to access employee e-mail, another section of the law specifies that "the person or entity providing a wire or electronic communications service" [6] is exempt from its restrictions. Since an employer that provides electronic mail falls within this exception, an employee will have no recourse under the ECPA to claim that he or she had a reasonable expectation of privacy. The case of *Andersen Consulting LLP v. UOP* [7] illustrates this point as applied in the independent contractor context.

Andersen, the plaintiff in this case, was a consulting firm hired by UOP to perform a system integration project. During the course of the project, Anderson's employees were given access to and used the UOP e-mail system. Subsequently, UOP terminated the project and sued Andersen for fraud, negligence, and breach of contract. During the litigation, UOP divulged the contents of Andersen's e-mail to *The Wall Street Journal*, which published an article entitled, "E-mail Trail Could Haunt

Consultants in Court." Andersen then sued for violation of a section of the ECPA that directs that "a person or entity providing an electronic communications service to the public shall not knowingly divulge to any person or entity the contents of its communications while in storage by the service" [8]. The court dismissed the suit on the grounds that UOP's internal e-mail system was not "public" and therefore UOP was free to access and reveal e-mail sent by Andersen employees using the system.

If employees can somehow establish that they had a reasonable expectation of privacy as to e-mail communications made using employer e-mail systems, state statutes and tort law may offer employees an alternative source of protection. Some states have privacy statutes that might apply; however, a suit under one such statute in California was unsuccessful. In *Shoars v. Epson America, Inc.* [9], Shoars, who was an e-mail administrator for Epson, was terminated after complaining about her supervisor's reading of employee e-mail messages. She sued under a California statute that prohibits electronic surveillance of employees. The court ruled that the statute was not intended to protect employee e-mail.

State tort law has recognized civil liability for invasion of privacy. One is liable for invasion of privacy when he or she unreasonably intrudes upon an area or the affairs of another person in which that person has a reasonable expectation of privacy. The key to proving this claim is proof that the plaintiff reasonably expected that the area in question was private. The plaintiff in *Smyth v. Pillsbury* [10] claimed he had been wrongfully discharged in violation of his right to privacy after Pillsbury had told employees that their e-mail was confidential and would not be used against them. Smyth had sent an e-mail to his supervisor referring to management as "those backstabbing bastards." In assessing Smyth's claim:

> [W]e do not find a reasonable expectation of privacy in e-mail communications voluntarily made by an employee to his supervisor over the company e-mail system notwithstanding any assurances that such communications would not be intercepted by management. Once the plaintiff communicated the alleged unprofessional comments to a second person (his supervisor) over an e-mail system which was apparently utilized by the entire company, any reasonable expectation of privacy was lost. Significantly, the defendant did not require the plaintiff, as in the case of an urinalysis or personal property search, to disclose any personal information about himself. Rather, the plaintiff voluntarily communi-

> cated the alleged unprofessional comments over the company e-mail system. We find no privacy interests in such communications.... Moreover, the company's interest in preventing inappropriate and unprofessional comments or even illegal activity over its e-mail system outweighs any privacy interest the employee may have in those comments [11].

Therefore, the court granted Pillsbury's motion to dismiss the case. As this case and the foregoing discussion suggest, employers appear to have wide latitude in regulating their e-mail systems.

Likewise, the court in *McLaren v. Microsoft Corp.* [12] reached the same result. McLaren, a Microsoft employee, was suspended from work pending an investigation into allegations of sexual harassment. He requested that no one access his e-mail and later sued, claiming that Microsoft invaded his privacy by breaking into the file folders labeled "personal" in which he stored his e-mail on the network. Even so, the court dismissed his claim after observing that the messages had already been transmitted over Microsoft's network and at that point were accessible to third parties. The court added: "[T]he company's interest in preventing inappropriate and unprofessional comments, or even illegal activity, over its email system would outweigh McLaren's claimed privacy interest in those communications" [13].

Although the foregoing discussion makes it unlikely, there is always a possibility that an employer may inadvertently create a work environment in which an employee can justifiably assert a reasonable expectation of privacy. For instance, if an employer assures employees that their e-mail would not be monitored or used as grounds for evaluation [14] *and* allowed employees to use its computers for personal use, then the employer may have created a reasonable expectation of privacy. It could be argued that an employee who uses his or her own laptop computer at work has a reasonable expectation that its contents are private. An employee who telecommutes from home might make a similar case. Since no courts have as yet addressed cases such as these, we can only speculate as to the scope of the employer's liability for invasion of privacy.

Crafting an employee e-mail use policy

In light of the legal principles and case law just discussed, an employer should take affirmative steps to minimize its exposure to liability for the consequences of employee misuse of e-mail and employee claims for invasion of privacy. The most effective approach is to adopt and disseminate to employees a written statement that clearly communicates the employer's policy regarding personal use of e-mail and that limits e-mail content to business purposes [15]. In particular, employers should give careful consideration to the following in putting in place such policies:

- The policy should be made widely available and emphasize that the e-mail system, both hardware and software, and all electronic communications are the property of the employer.
- The employer should make clear in the policy that the e-mail system is made available for business and work-related purposes only, and that use of e-mail for personal or other uses is considered a violation of the policy.
- The employee should be instructed by the policy that no e-mail is considered to be private and confidential, unless necessary to protect information considered proprietary or sensitive by the employer.
- The policy should remind employees that e-mail may be used as evidence in lawsuits [16] and that content that amounts to defamation, sexual or racial harassment, or copyright infringement may lead to legal liability for the employer and, quite possibly, the employee as well.

As to implementation, the employer should require a signed acknowledgment from each employee that he or she has received and read the policy [17]. Employers should issue all e-mail passwords and prevent employees from using passwords unknown to the employer. It is also advisable to secure the e-mail system by using firewalls or encryption for e-mail containing trade secrets or other information considered to be confidential in nature.

Employers should also seriously consider monitoring e-mail to enforce these restrictions. E-mail monitoring in the workplace may seem like an extraordinary means of enforcing an e-mail policy, but a growing number of businesses do this on a regular basis. A 1999 survey by the American Management Association found that 27% of all U.S. companies now monitor employee e-mail [18]. Recall that should the employee challenge a disciplinary action or termination in court, the court will be most concerned with whether the employee had a reasonable expectation of privacy in e-mail. In such a case, employers that can produce a written e-mail use policy and justify monitoring as a means of ensuring compliance with policy will be in a stronger position on defense than those who cannot do so. They can prove that the employee did not have a reasonable expectation of privacy and that the employer had legitimate, business-related reason for monitoring and taking action against the employee.

If an employer chooses to monitor, then employees should be given notice in writing that the employer may review e-mail at any time and for any reason without prior warning to the employee. A formal e-mail use policy, along with warning that actual monitoring occurs, allow an employer to control its e-mail system, while laying the groundwork for later disciplining or terminating an employee who abuses it. Furthermore, if monitoring is part of an employer's overall policy, it is important that it be done consistently in order to be of maximum protection to the employer and to prevent charges of employment discrimination [19].

While an e-mail use policy can shield an employer from the legal risks discussed in this chapter, a policy that is too heavy handed may carry a risk as well. As a matter of fairness and good faith, employees deserve to know the full extent to which their e-mail and computer use will be monitored so that they will not be unfairly surprised later on if a problem arises. In addition, employers should consider the effect on employee morale and satisfaction. Indeed, in a competitive employment market, an unreasonably oppressive policy may dissuade potential job applicants or encourage employee turnover. Likewise, employers may want to assess the ethical considerations involved when adopting a policy [20] and consider the potential effect on employee productivity when draconian policies are put in place.

In sum, this chapter and the foregoing suggestions address important concerns that arise when employees use e-mail; however, they should form only one part of an overall employer computer use policy. Finally, other legal issues along these lines are certain to arise as more employees opt to telecommute from home, using their own or employer-provided computers, and as other digital communication technologies are adapted to use in the workplace.

Endnotes

[1] 751 A.2d 538 (2000).

[2] An anologous case is *Strauss v. Microsoft Corp.*, 68 Fair Empl. Prac. Cases (BNA) 1576 (S.D.N.Y. 1995), in which the plaintiff, a female employee who was passed over for a promotion and then dismissed, sued Microsoft for sex discrimination. She alleged that her supervisor sexually harassed her by making certain derogatory remarks to her in e-mail. The court stated that the e-mail messages, when viewed in the light of Strauss' other evidence, could lead a reasonable jury to conclude that Microsoft engaged in discrimination.

[3] No. 99-55106 (C.D. Cal. 2001).

[4] See *Burdeau v. McDowell*, 256 U.S. 465 (1921).

[5] 18 U.S.C. § 2701(a)(2).

[6] 18 U.S.C. § 2701(c)(1).

[7] F. Supp. (N.D. Ill. 1998).

[8] 18 U.S.C. § 2702(a)(1).

[9] 1994 Cal. LEXIS 3670 (Cal. S. Ct. June 29, 1994).

[10] 914 F. Supp. 97 (E.D. Pa. 1996).

[11] *Id.* at 101.

[12] 1999 Tex. App. LEXIS 4103 (Tex. Ct. App. 1999).

[13] *Id.*

[14] Recall that assurances such as these, standing alone, were not enough in the *Smyth* case to create a reasonable expectation of privacy.

[15] The Electronic Mail Association has published a useful resource book that provides information for preparing a workplace e-mail policy and contains a number of sample policy provisions. See Electronic Mail Association, "Privacy Tool Kit: Access to and Use and Disclosure of Electronic Mail on Company Computer Systems. A Guide to Formulating Your Company's Policy," 1999. For further information about the organization and this publication, see http://www.ema.org/restricted/documents/index.htm.

[16] E-mail evidence, for instance, played a key role in the antitrust litigation against Microsoft. See also *Greenslade v. Chicago Sun-Times*, 112 F.3d 853 (7th Cir. 1997) (e-mail evidence used to prove that job transfer was not disciminatory); *Harley v. McCoach*, 928 F. Supp. 533 (E.D. Pa. 1996) (hostile work environment evidenced by e-mail containing racist

messages); *Strauss v. Microsoft*, 814 F. Supp. 1186 (S.D.N.Y. 1995) (court considered e-mail messages as relevant and probative evidence).

[17] For a sample e-mail and Internet use policy, see www.giglaw.com/library/e-mailpolicy.html.

[18] Seglin, J. L., "You've Got Mail. You're Being Watched," *New York Times*, July 18, 1999, at www.nytimes.com/library/tech/99/07/biztech/articles/18ethics.html.

[19] See *Miller v. U.S.F. & G.*, 65 F.E.P. Cas. (BNA) 593 (D. Md. 1994) (inconsistent enforcement may be a basis for employment discrimination suit).

[20] See Doss, E. and M. C. Loui, "Ethics and the Privacy of Electronic Mail," *The Information Society*, Vol. 11, 1995, p. 223 (discussing the ethical aspects of privacy intrusions).

8

Detection and deterrence of on-line crime

Computer crime is any conduct that employs information technology to accomplish an illegal purpose. Brought about by the borderless nature of cyberspace and the seamlessness of interlinked computer networks, businesses and law enforcement officials face novel issues when it comes to crime in the information era [1]. Collecting and using personal data such as names, addresses, phone numbers, personal characteristics, financial information, medical history, and other personal background and identifying facts, makes storage, retrieval, and use of such information more efficient and easily accessible. Electronic data collection and use involve concerns about security and confidentiality. Electronic databases containing such information can be vulnerable to hacking or criminal misuse.

Moreover, access to computers and to the Internet is relatively easy and inexpensive, and the ability to victimize a huge number of people and businesses is virtually unlimited. The potential magnitude of the problem has been summarized as follows:

> Before the advent of computer networks, the ability to steal information or damage property was to some extent determined by physical limitations. A burglar could only break into so many windows and burglarize so many homes in a week. During each intrusion, he could take away only what he could carry. While this conduct is by no means trivial, the amount of property he could steal or the amount of damage he could cause was restricted by physical limitations. In the information age, these limitations no longer apply. Criminals seeking information stored in networked computers with dial-in access can access that information from virtually anywhere in the world. The quantity of information that can be stolen, or the amount of damage that can be caused by malicious programming code, may be limited only by the speed of the network and the criminal's equipment [2].

As such, the challenge posed by on-line crime is hard to understate. Preexisting criminal laws and traditional law enforcement strategies may be largely ineffective at detecting the perpetrators or punishing such conduct. This chapter considers the roles of computers and the Internet in the commission of crime, and outlines the applicable laws with particular emphasis on federal statutes. Finally, a number of strategies and safeguards to prevent computer crimes will be proposed.

Criminal conduct involving computers and the Internet

A perpetrator can use computers to conceal his or her true identity, or to enhance the severity and efficiency of the criminal offense committed. Essentially, computers have played two primary roles in criminal conduct. First, a computer network can be the target of criminal activity. Second, a computer can be the instrument used to facilitate the crime.

A computer can be the target of a crime when the perpetrator utilizes the computer to hack or gain access to data or programs stored on the computer without authorization. The purpose is to steal information stored on the system, to gain control of the system, or to sabotage or alter the integrity of stored data. The perpetrator may want to misappropriate trade secrets or other proprietary information, copy data or programs protected by copyright, introduce a virus into the system, or conceal his or her identity in order to launch an attack on another system.

A computer can be a tool for committing a crime on-line. A perpetrator might use the Internet to distribute and receive child pornography; copy and distribute copyrighted or proprietary files or programs; harass, threaten, defraud, or stalk others; spread viruses or worms; vandalize Web sites; or post false or misleading information. Similarly, the perpetrator might use a computer to transmit classified government information, sell controlled items such as drugs or firearms, engage in hate speech, disrupt services, or disable systems. Some of these acts may be committed using e-mail and on-line bulletin boards or chatrooms [3].

Obviously, these categories overlap in that the perpetration of a criminal act against one computer or network may involve the use of another computer as a tool of the act. There are seemingly innumerable possible opportunities to exploit existing technology and to take advantage of security vulnerabilities when it comes to on-line crime. The global nature of the Internet has also posed a unique problem regarding investigation and prosecution of cybercrimes that might be committed across international borders, stimulating the need for transnational cooperation and coordination. For instance, the Council of Europe Convention on Cybercrime seeks to harmonize criminal substantive and procedural laws that define computer crimes, and promote international coordination of transnational criminal prosecutions [4].

On the domestic front, the federal and state governments have responded to these challenges with new laws and enforcement efforts. The United States Department of Justice has established a separate computer crime section, while the FBI maintains a center for investigating cybercrime and assessing its threat to national security. There is also President's Working Group on Unlawful Conduct on the Internet chaired by the attorney general [5]. Likewise, in recent years all of the states have adopted statutes to combat on-line crime. Many of these statutes mirror their federal counterparts, while some of these statutes predate federal legislation. Federal laws that define and punish on-line crime will be considered in the next section.

Federal control of on-line crime

Most existing state and federal laws apply with equal force in the electronic environment and do not distinguish between illegal acts committed on-line or off-line. Thus, laws prohibiting extortion, gambling, consumer fraud, securities fraud, and identity theft, among others, remain operative. Several federal statutes have been enacted that specifically address on-line crime in interstate commerce. One of the first and arguably most important federal statutes enacted to criminalize certain on-line misconduct was the Computer Fraud and Abuse Act [6], which is intended to protect the confidentiality, integrity, and availability of computer data and communications. The act prohibits the use of computers to

- Knowingly commit espionage by accessing information without authorization or exceeding authorized access;
- Access other information without authorization or exceeding authorized access;
- Access any nonpublic government computer;
- Access any computer with an intent to commit fraud;
- Knowingly or intentionally damage a computer;
- Knowingly traffic in computer passwords;
- Threaten to cause damage to a computer with the intent to extort money or other items of value.

The Computer Fraud and Abuse Act may also be used along with other criminal statutes when the crimes committed have made use of computers. This statute was applied in the case of *United States v. Morris* [7], in which a graduate computer science student at Cornell University released a worm onto the Internet as part of an experiment to prove the inadequacies of on-line security measures to guard against computer viruses. The worm was meant to be innocuous, but it spread more rapidly than he had planned, causing numerous computers, as well as university, military, and government systems, to crash. Morris was charged and convicted of intentionally accessing a government computer without authorization under the Computer Fraud and Abuse Act because the worm he created was designed to enter computers to which he had no permission to use.

The federal wire fraud statute has also been invoked to combat on-line fraud. Wire fraud is defined as a “scheme to defraud by means of false pretenses" that involves the "defendant's knowing and willful participation in the scheme with intent to defraud" and "the use of interstate wire communications in furtherance of the scheme" [8]. The defendant in *United States v. Riggs* [9] was charged with using his home computer to gain unauthorized access to a computer owned by Bell South Telephone in order to download a file describing its 911 system. Riggs posted the file on an on-line bulletin board using an interstate computer network. The court held that he had employed fraudulent means to gain access to Bell South's system and then attempted to disguise his identity in violation of the wire fraud statute.

Likewise, in *United States v. Czubinski* [10], the defendant, an employee of the Internal Revenue Service (IRS), was charged under the wire fraud statute. Using his password and certain search codes, the defendant accessed the tax returns of several individuals stored on the IRS computer database. There was no evidence that he disclosed or sold the information to any third parties. Consequently, the court found that wire fraud could not be proved since there was no evidence of an underlying scheme to defraud, which is a necessary element of proof. In other cases, the courts have found violations of the wire fraud statute when defendants misappropriated confidential source code and software by interstate wire transmission [11]. Additionally, the Electronic Funds Transfer Act [12] criminalizes the provision of false, inaccurate, or insufficient information with respect to the use of electronic funds transfer systems. This statute also prohibits any electronic transactions involving counterfeit, stolen, fictitious debt instruments, including codes, cards, or similar means used to effect an electronic funds transfer.

Several federal statutes also prohibit electronic piracy of intellectual property. For instance, the No Electronic Theft Act proscribes the willful reproduction or distribution of copyrighted works by electronic means, even where the perpetrator incurs no financial gain from doing so [13]. Similarly, the Economic Espionage Act prohibits the theft or misappropriation of trade secrets by a computer [14]. The act seeks to prevent trade secret espionage that benefits foreign governments as well. In *United States v. Hsu* [15], for example, the defendant was prosecuted for economic espionage when he attempted to acquire the formulas and processes for making an anticancer drug protected by Bristol-Myers as trade secrets.

Aside from conduct that has resulted in authorized access and theft, federal laws have been invoked to prosecute on-line threats and obscenity.

For instance, federal legislation outlaws the interstate or foreign transmission of communications involving kidnapping, extortion, or threats to injure another person [16]. A University of Michigan student was charged under this statute in 1995 after he posted a story on an on-line newsgroup, describing a sexually violent fantasy involving a fellow student. He had also transmitted e-mail regarding this story to a third student. The federal district court, however, dismissed the charges on the grounds that his communication was not an "unequivocal, unconditional, immediate and specific" threat directed against the female student [17]. This type of on-line harassment or "cyberstalking" has now been outlawed by most states [18]. Indeed, in the case of *People v. Kochanowski* [19], the court held that a Web site that encouraged Internet users to make sexually suggestive phone calls to the defendant's ex-girlfriend constituted harassment.

Federal law also forbids the interstate transportation for commercial purposes of any lewd, lascivious book, or any other indecent or immoral material [20]. In the case of *United States v. Thomas* [21], the California defendants operated an on-line bulletin board service where subscribers could upload and download pornographic images. A Tennessee postal inspector subscribed to their service and downloaded several sexually explicit images. The defendants were then charged with and convicted of transporting obscene material in interstate commerce. On appeal, the court upheld the application of the obscenity laws to electronic transmissions [22].

Computer technology has also given another obscenity statute a wider interpretation by at least one court. The Child Pornography Prevention Act criminalizes the knowing sale, possession, or distribution of child pornography in interstate commerce by any means, including computers. In *United States v. Hilton* [23], the defendant challenged the constitutionality of this statute after he was arrested for possession of computer disks containing pictures of children. Hilton argued that the statute was an overly broad restraint on free speech because the statute was being applied to not only to forbid images of actual children, but also to prohibit an image that "appears to be a minor." The court disagreed, holding that the law was not an unconstitutional extension of prior law because it is now possible that computerized image of "an innocent picture of a child may be manipulated by computer to create a sexually-oriented photo, or a fake child...can be generated wholly by computer graphics" [24].

Defendant's constitutional rights in criminal investigations

While the focus of this chapter is the detection and deterrence of Internet and computer crime, it is worth reviewing the rights of one accused of an on-line crime under the United States Constitution. The Fourth Amendment to the U.S. Constitution declares that "the right of the people to be secure in their persons, houses, papers, and effects, against unreasonable search and seizures, shall not be violated" [25]. Before the government can seize a person's property, a court must issue a valid search warrant based on probable cause. In other words, the authorities must have sound reasons to believe that the instrumentalities or other evidence of a crime are present at the location to be searched. If probable cause is lacking, then any evidence seized will be inadmissible in the criminal proceedings that follow [26].

In *United States v. Carey* [27], the court held that a police officer's search of computer file violated the Fourth Amendment. Although the officer had a warrant authorizing a search of computer files for information related to drug trafficking, he discovered a file containing child pornography and began searching for similar files. Nonetheless, the court invalidated the search because it exceeded the scope of the warrant when the officer began looking for child pornography files. By contrast, the court in *United States v. Campos* [28] held that a search warrant for computer hardware that was based on evidence that the hardware was used to transmit two files containing child pornography. When the officer found other such files, the defendant argued that the Fourth Amendment precluded admission of these files into evidence at his trial. The court disagreed on the grounds that the scope of the search was not unreasonably expanded since the warrant was directed at finding evidence of child pornography, and it was necessary to search other files to find them.

The Fourth Amendment applies with equal force to individuals and businesses, so that a business' property is afforded the same protection. If law enforcement officials conduct an unreasonable search by failing to obtain a valid warrant or by impermissibly exceeding the scope of the warrant, then any evidence obtained during the search is not admissible at trial. Thus, all business records, as well as computer files, data, software, and hardware, are guaranteed the protection of the Fourth Amendment in a criminal investigation.

Preventing computer crime and criminal culpability

We have seen that cybercriminals can attack computer systems and victimize businesses and computers using a variety of illegal acts, ranging from piracy of proprietary information, interception and alteration of data, hacking, fraud, and viruses. While no preventative strategies will be completely foolproof, it is strongly advisable to take all reasonable steps to prevent on-line crime before it happens, if for no other reason than to avoid criminal culpability for the crime itself. Clearly, businesses that initiate and perpetrate a cybercrime will be primarily culpable for that crime, though a business that knows of illegal activities on its system but does nothing to stop them can be charged with facilitating or aiding and abetting the crime. Moreover, while lack of criminal intent to commit a crime or knowledge of criminal activity does not usually give rise to liability, lack of knowledge will *not* necessarily be a defense if the business suspects that criminal activity is afoot but does nothing to investigate [29]. Some simple safeguards that should be considered include the following:

- Install devices such as highly secure firewalls, password protection systems, and access use and monitoring software to protect databases containing confidential, sensitive, or proprietary data, as well as information or materials that are protected by copyright or trade secret.
- Conduct regular internal audits of the system.
- Implement acceptable use policies as to what is considered permissible employee use and misuse of computers, define clearly what constitutes misuse and illegal use in such policies, and regularly monitor employees for compliance with the policies.
- Require system users to change passwords frequently and use complex alphanumeric passwords.
- Install intrusion detection software.
- Encrypt sensitive and proprietary data and communications.
- Act immediately if it is discovered that an employee has misused a computer for illegal purposes by terminating or suspending the employee and changing access codes that may have been compromised.

If your business is the target of a computer crime, immediately collect all system access and use records, including user login and logout times, file uploads and downloads, e-mail sent or collected, files accessed and programs used, and Web sites visited [30]. Finally, immediately contact the law enforcement authorities and cooperate fully with them to investigate the intrusion or misconduct [31].

Endnotes

[1] For various accounts of crimes committed and investigated in cyberspace, see Hafner, K., and J. Markoff, *Cyberpunk: Outlaws and Hackers on the Computer Frontier,* Seattle, WA: Touchstone Books, 1995; Markoff, J., and T. Shimomuru, *Takedown: The Pursuit and Capture of Kevin Mitnick, America's Most Wanted Computer Outlaw by the Man Who Did It,* New York: Hyperion Books, 1996; Sterling, B., *The Hacker Crackdown: Law and Disorder on the Electronic Frontier,* 1993, http://www.eff.org/pub/Publications/Bruce_Sterling/Hacker_Crackdown/Hacker_Crackdown_HTML/.

[2] Charney, S. and K. Alexander, "Computer Crime," *Emory Law. J.,* Vol. 45, 1996, pp. 931, 940, 1996.

[3] In addition, a computer may be *incidental* to the commission of a crime in the sense that, while the computer is not the victim or instrumentality of the crime, it is used for record-keeping or communications. A criminal might use a computer to record and store names, dates, amounts, addresses, credit card numbers, and similar information related to his or her illegal activities. For instance, an identity thief might store lists of stolen credit card or Social Security numbers on a computer.

[4] The Convention is available at conventions.coe.int/treaty/EN/projets/CyberRapex7.htm. See also U.S. Department of Justice, "Frequently Asked Questions and Answers About the Council of Europe Convention on Cybercrime," Dec. 1, 2000, www.doj.gov/criminal/cybercrime/COEFAQs.htm.

[5] The Working Group has produced a comprehensive report and set of recommendations. See "The Electronic Frontier: The Challenge of Unlawful Conduct Involving Use of the Internet," 2000, http://www.usdoj.gov/criminal/cybercrime/unlawful.htm.

[6] 18 U.S.C. § 1030(a).

[7] 928 F.2d 504 (2d Cir. 1991).

[8] 18 U.S.C. § 1343.

[9] 739 F. Supp. 414 (N.D. Ill. 1990).

[10] 106 F.3d 1069 (1st Cir. 1997).

[11] See, *e.g., United States v. Wang*, 898 F. Supp. 758 (D. Colo. 1995) (source code); *United States v. Seidlitz*, 589 F.2d 152 (4th Cir. 1978) (software).

[12] 15 U.S.C. § 1693n.

[13] 17 U.S.C. § 506(a).

[14] 18 U.S.C. § 1831.

[15] 155 F.3d 189 (3d Cir. 1998).

[16] 18 U.S.C. § 875.

[17] *United States v. Baker*, 890 F. Supp. 1375, 1382 (E.D. Mich. 1995).

[18] *E.g., Cal. Penal Code* § 646.9 (West 1998); *Conn. Gen. Stat. Ann.* § 53a-181d (West 1994); *Fla. Stat. Ann* § 784.048 (West 1998).

[19] No. 99-1711 DCR (N.Y. Sup. Ct. 2000)

[20] 18 U.S.C. § 1460 *et seq.*

[21] 74 F.3d 701 (6th Cir. 1996).

[22] Other similar statutes have not survived constitutional scrutiny. The Communications Decency Act, which prohibited on-line transmission of "indecent" materials, was ruled unconstitutionally vague and overbroad under the First Amendment in *Reno v. ACLU*, 521 U.S. 844 (1997). The Child On-line Protection Act, which forbade commercial transmission of material that is "harmful to minors," was struck down for similar reasons in *ACLU v. Reno*, 31 F. Supp.2d 473 (E.D. Pa. 1999).

[23] 167 F.3d 61 (1st Cir. 1999).

[24] *Id.* But see *Free Speech Coalition v. Reno*, 1999 U.S. App. LEXIS 32704 (Dec. 17, 1999) (holding that the First Amendment forbids criminalization of completely computerized images of fictitious children engaged in imaginary but sexually explicit conduct).

[25] *U.S. Const.* amend IV.

[26] There are several exceptions to the requirement of a valid warrant. For instance, a law enforcement official may seize property that can be seen in the open by others if the official suspects that the property is evidence of criminal activity. This is known as the "plain view" exception.

[27] 172 F.3d 1268 (10th Cir. 1999).

[28] No. 99-5050 (10th Cir. 2000).

[29] Even if a business knows of but fails to act to stop or prevent illegal acts on its system, it may nonetheless face civil tort liability for its inaction.

[30] For guidance in investigating on-line crime, see Wright, T. E., "The Field Guide for Investigating Computer Crime," www.securityfocus.com/focus/ih/articles/crimeguide1.htm.

[31] Consider also reporting the situation to the Computer Emergency Response Team (CERT), based at the Software Engineering Institute at Carnegie Mellon University and found on-line at http://www.cert.org. CERT promotes the exchange of information regarding security intrusions and prevention of cybercrime.

9

Software and Internet patent protection

Once a backwater in the realm of on-line intellectual property protection, patent law has taken center stage alongside copyright and trademark rights. A patent is a grant issued by the federal government that gives an inventor the right to exclude all others from making, using, or selling the invention within the United States, its territories, and possessions for a period of 20 years. Patents on computer-related inventions now play a crucial role in securing a competitive advantage in the electronic marketplace. More recently, the patentability of business methods has been reaffirmed, setting off a scramble among firms to secure patent protection for a variety of Internet-based business systems and technologies. Patents are certain to further shape the nature of electronic commerce and define the bounds of on-line competition for years to come.

Any business engaged in developing software or doing business on the Internet should know its rights and potential liabilities under patent law. Another increasingly important consideration is the potential to enhance revenues through the licensing of software and business method patents. A related concern to on-line businesses is the liability for infringement claims brought by owners of such patents, some of whom may be competitors. This chapter provides an overview of the requirements for patentability and the scope of patent protection available for software and Internet-related inventions. Practical suggestions for addressing the opportunities and concerns presented by patents are offered as well.

Patentability requirements and patent infringement

As with copyrights, the United States Constitution allows Congress the authority to protect inventors by granting them certain exclusive rights in their inventions in the form of a patent. A patent represents an incentive to would-be inventors to invest the time and energy necessary to research and develop their inventions. As such, the patent is a bargain between an inventor and the government. The government grants the inventor these exclusive rights in exchange for fully disclosing the invention to the public in the patent application. Thus, like a copyright, a patent is a government-sanctioned limited monopoly. Congress has enacted the Patent Act, which spells out the requirements for patent protection in the United States. The responsibility of examining patent applications and granting patents rests with by the United States Patent & Trademark Office (USPTO).

The process of gaining patent protection begins with the inventor, who must apply for and be granted a patent on his or her invention. The application contains claims that must describe in detail the invention for which protection is sought. Once filed, a USPTO patent examiner reviews the application to determine whether the invention meets the standards for patentability. To qualify for patent protection, the invention must meet four distinct requirements. It must be of the type of subject matter that may be protected, and it must be useful, novel, and nonobvious [1].

- *Patentable subject matter:* The Patent Act specifies five categories of inventions that may be patented: processes, machines, manufactures, compositions of matter, and improvements to any of these. A process is a method or series of operations for producing a concrete result. A machine is a mechanical device that performs a function or yields a result, while a manufacture is an article made by humans or machines by adding, assembling, or rearranging its elements. Compositions of matter involve intermixtures of ingredients. Finally, any new uses for any of the above may be patented as well.

- *Utility:* The invention must be useful, not merely theoretical. An invention is useful if it is operable and has a purpose that is beneficial to society. Almost any type of utility will meet this requirement [2].
- *Novelty:* The invention must be new; that is, it must be something that no one else has publicly made or used before in the United States, or patented or described in a printed publication anywhere else. This conclusion is made by looking to the body of prior inventions, discoveries, and published research (known as the prior art) and determining whether the invention contains at least one element or component that does not exist within any single source or reference in the prior art.
- *Nonobviousness:* The invention must not be obvious to a person having ordinary skill in the art and who understands the technical field of the invention so that it represents an inventive next step or significant development in the art. An invention will be considered obvious when there is at least one reference, whether in the prior art or in the knowledge of those with ordinary skill in the art, suggesting that it would be desirable to improve the reference or to combine the features of two or more references. The prior art references also must suggest a reasonable expectation that the improvement or combination will be successful.

These requirements are highly technical and the USPTO patent examiner will closely analyze the invention and the prior art to see if each requirement is met. If the claimed invention meets each of these standards, a patent will be issued to the inventor. Under the Patent Act, a patentee has the right to exclude all others from making, using, or selling the protected invention for 20 years [3]. A patent owner may bring an infringement action in a federal court against anyone who uses, makes, or sells the invention without permission. If successful, the patent owner may obtain an injunction, which orders the infringer to cease any further use or sale of the infringing device, and which awards damages to the patent owner [4]. To determine if a defendant is infringing a patent, a court will read the claims describing the plaintiff's device or process and compare them with the elements of the defendant's device or process. If the claims of the allegedly infringing device are literally the same as or substantially equivalent to the plaintiff's, then an infringement has occurred.

Patent protection in foreign countries

Laws governing the patentability of inventions and application filing procedures vary from country to country. A U.S. patent is valid within the United States, but if an inventor wanted also to patent his or her invention in Japan or Germany, the inventor would need to apply for a patent in Japan or Germany. The patent laws of other countries differ as to procedures for filing for and obtaining a patent, and as to what types of inventions may be protected. Some countries will deny a patent to an inventor if he or she has publicly disclosed the invention before filing a patent application, whereas the United States allows the inventor up to one year to file a patent application after he or she has first publicly disclosed the invention, published information about it, or offered it for sale. Additionally, in most other countries, if the patentability requirements are met, the first inventor to file an application receives the patent, though an invention is unpatentable unless a patent application is filed before publication of the invention or discovery. By contrast, the United States maintains a "first to invent" patent system that grants the patent on a device or process to the person who can prove that he or she was the first inventor, irrespective of whether that person is the first to apply for a patent.

Two international treaties, of which the United States is a signatory, are in place to facilitate the patent application process for inventors who seek patent protection in more than one country. Under the Paris Convention [5], an inventor may file a patent application in one country, and then file a patent application in a second country within one year of filing in the first country. This allows the inventor to claim priority of invention, using the filing date of the first application. The Patent Cooperation Treaty [6] permits an inventor to file an international patent application, which delays the time by which the inventor must file later patent applications in other countries by as much as 30 months. Under the treaty, the inventor obtains a filing date that every other signatory country will recognize, though the inventor must eventually file separate patent applications in each country. As of yet, there is no form of universal patent protection that would apply in all countries, though the Europe Union maintains a regional patent system. The European Patent Office (EPO) can grant patents that are enforceable in most European countries. This step may presage future efforts to develop a worldwide patent.

Patentability of computer-related inventions

The United States Court of Appeals for the Federal Circuit is the court that hears all appeals involving patent validity and infringement. Its decisions are appealable only to the United States Supreme Court. Together with the Supreme Court, the Federal Circuit has held that inventions relating to computer programs, the Internet, and methods of doing business are patentable subject matter. In the aftermath of these decisions, the number of patents issued on such inventions has skyrocketed. Along with this development is a growing amount of patent infringement litigation. The following is an overview of the current approach to the scope of patent protection in this area.

Computer programs

An abstract idea or a mathematical equation, such as the Pythagorean theorem, is not patentable subject matter for the reason that a patent on the equation would effectively preempt all others from using it without the permission of the patent owner. Since early computers did little more than solve complex mathematical equations, the Patent Office and the courts traditionally refused to grant patents on software. By 1969, the USPTO had begun to grant patents on computer programs. In the 1972 case of *Gottshalk v. Benson* [7], however, the Supreme Court invalidated a patent on a program that used an algorithm to convert binary-coded decimal numbers into pure binary numbers, on the grounds that in allowing a patent on the program "the practical effect would be a patent on the algorithm itself" [8].

Following *Gottshalk*, the patenting of computer software slowed and many software developers turned instead to copyright protection for their applications. In 1981, the Supreme Court revisited the issue in the case of *Diamond v. Diehr* [9] and allowed a patent on a programmed computer, though not on the program itself. The Court explained that when "a claim containing a mathematical formula implements or applies that formula in a structure or process that, when considered as a whole, is...transforming or reducing an article to a different state or thing, then the claim satisfies the requirements of [the Patent Act]" [10].

In the years following the *Diehr* decision, the USPTO and the Federal Circuit Court of Appeals attempted in a series of cases to define when a computer-related process was directed to the *application* of a mathematical algorithm [11]. In 1996, in order to bring some clarity to this issue, the

Federal Office issued its *Examination Guidelines for Computer-Related Inventions* [12]. The guidelines provide a framework to assist patent examiners and attorneys in evaluating the patentability of software claims. Inventions that function under operation of software, or software that operates a computer, or a series of steps to be performed with a computer, are patentable. Compilations of data, algorithms without practical application, and processes consisting solely of steps to solve a mathematical problem or merely transform numbers from one type to another, are not patentable. Today, the patentability of software is well established, although the principle that a purely abstract algorithm is not patentable subject matter still holds true. If the program merely solves a mathematical equation or manipulates data or an abstract idea, then it is unpatentable. On the other hand, if the program performs these processes with a practical application or result, it may be patented [13].

Internet business methods

When the full potential of the Internet as a medium of commerce was finally realized in the mid-1990s, the spotlight of patent protection for information technology shifted to Internet-based inventions. Initially, there were doubts as to whether methods of doing business on-line could be patented or whether they amounted to little more than unpatentable mathematical algorithms. In the 1998 landmark case of *State Street Bank v. Signature Financial Group, Inc.* [14], the Federal Circuit Court of Appeals addressed this question and effectively eliminated any doubt that Internet-based business systems and models are patentable subject matter.

In the *State Street Bank* case, Signature Financial Group owned a patent directed to a data processing system for performing financial calculations and managing information for its investment and financial services business. State Street challenged the validity of the patent on the grounds that it was not patentable subject matter [15]. The district court held that Signature's invention involved a process solely of mathematical operations and was, therefore, unpatentable as a mathematical algorithm. On appeal, the Federal Circuit reversed, holding that "the question of whether a claim is directed to statutory subject matter should focus on the essential characteristics of the subject matter, particularly its practical utility" [16]. The court reasoned that if a process or a machine that has been programmed to implement a process produces a useful, concrete, and tangible result, then it is patentable subject matter, even if the useful result is a numerical expression, "such as profit, percentage, cost, or loss" [17].

As such, inventions that involve algorithms related to the operation of Internet-based businesses are plainly eligible for patent protection. Since the *State Street Bank* decision, the USPTO has issued numerous patents on Internet business models and systems, including methods for delivering advertising, coupons, and maps on the Internet, as well as systems for trading securities, transmitting digital video and audio signals, and shopping for consumer products [18]. Inevitably, the patentability of business methods was tested again and, in 1999, the Federal Circuit Court of Appeals reaffirmed its *State Street Bank* holding in the case of *AT&T Corp. v. Excel Communications, Inc.* [19]. This case involved a patent for a computerized method for generating billing information for long distance telephone calls. The district court had ruled that the patent was invalid because it recited merely a mathematical algorithm and was thus not patentable subject matter. The Federal Circuit again stated that a patent claim that recites a practical application of a mathematical algorithm by producing a useful, concrete, and tangible result is patentable subject matter under the Patent Act, regardless of whether the claimed invention is a product or a process [20].

The decisions in *State Street Bank* and *AT&T* have been followed by a number of high-profile infringement suits directed at on-line business methods [21]. Amazon.com brought one of the first such suits against Barnes & Noble, its chief competitor in the on-line book sales market. Within a month after Amazon.com had been granted a patent on its "1-Click" shopping method for placing purchase orders on the Internet, Amazon.com sued Barnes & Noble to bar it from infringing the 1-Click system through Barnes & Noble's "Express Lane" on-line shopping feature. Barnes & Noble challenged the validity of the 1-Click patent, arguing that the patent was invalid due to several existing systems that had been in prior public use and a prior U.S. patent that were not considered by the USPTO during examination of the 1-Click patent. The federal district court concluded that nothing in the prior art anticipated or made obvious the 1-Click method. Thus, the court was persuaded to issue an injunction against Barnes & Noble [22]. Barnes & Noble then filed an appeal with the Federal Circuit Court of Appeals. The court vacated the injunction and remanded the case for further proceedings after concluding that Amazon.com was likely to be able to prove infringement if its patent was able to withstand a challenge to its validity on the obviousness grounds [23].

The issue of *obviousness* that Barnes & Noble raised as potential bar to the patenting of some Internet-based business methods will remain an ongoing concern to Internet businesses. Meeting the nonobviousness requirement for patentability might be problematic when real-world business methods are applied or adapted to the Internet. For instance, an inventory control system that has been used in the real world for many years, but that is performed on an Internet shopping Web site, may meet the novelty requirement if no single prior art reference discloses such an Internet-based system. Nonetheless, the inventory control system may not meet the nonobviousness requirement if applying it to an Internet shopping Web site would not yield an unexpected result or represent a technical leap that was unforeseeable by those skilled in developing electronic business models or designing the software to implement such systems. The problem presented to a firm sued for infringement of an Internet business method patent is whether it is possible to find any prior art that could invalidate the patent. The USPTO has acknowledged this issue and has begun to subject business method patent applications to greater scrutiny [24]. For instance, the USPTO plans to expand its prior art searches and institute a second level of review for such patent applications. One result of these efforts may be that the flood of business method patents may slow somewhat. Meanwhile, the pool of prior art that the USPTO and those who have been sued for infringement will examine is certain to expand [25].

International approaches to software and business method patents

The proliferation of software and business method patents in the United States has been felt abroad as well. Aside from the United States, Japan and Europe are the other principal centers of technological development and patenting. The Japanese Patent Office has recognized that computer-related inventions that use or are applied by hardware to solve a problem may be patented. Under the Japanese patent law, software may be patented, and business methods that utilize computer hardware for problem solving will be treated as patentable inventions as well [26]. By contrast, the European Patent Office, based on article 52(2)(c) of the European Patent Convention, does not allow patents on software or business methods. The U.K. Patent Office has reached a similar conclusion as to the unpatentability of Internet business methods under British law [27]. Given the growing importance of software and business method patents, as well as the number of U.S. patents on software and business models issued to American, Japanese, and European firms and software developers, it is likely that European firms will push to gain similar protection in Europe as well. In the meantime, U.S. firms doing business in European countries should be aware that their software and business method inventions will not qualify for the same patent protection available under United States law.

Considerations as to computer-related patent protection

The legal developments discussed in this chapter, as well as current trends in the law and electronic commerce, present on-line businesses and software developers with several challenges. Obviously, a firm should always consider the possibility of protecting its technology through patent protection. The assessment of whether it is wise to apply for a patent, and the patent application process, is complex and highly technical and should be undertaken using patent counsel. It is wise to adopt a patent policy to guide inventive activities and define ownership of any resulting patent rights. For example, an employee who invents a patentable computer program or business method is the owner of the patent, even though the invention may have been researched and developed using employer resources, materials, facilities, and other employees. To ensure that the employer is allowed to make, use, and sell the invention without paying unreasonable royalties to the employee-inventor, and to preclude the employee from refusing to license the invention or licensing it to a competitor, the employer and employee should execute an invention assignment agreement. Such an agreement requires that the employee shall disclose all potentially patentable inventions or discoveries, and then agree to file a patent application with the USPTO, usually with the assistance of the employer. In addition, it is customary that the employee agrees to assign the patent rights to the employer, or grant the employer an exclusive license to make, use, and sell the invention in the United States and elsewhere.

Another reason for implementing a patent policy is to document the invention and discovery process. Inventors should keep accurate records of their activities during the research process so as to document the dates on which the invention was conceived and made workable. This can be done by keeping journals or notebooks, which are dated, signed, and witnessed on a regular basis. Doing this allows the inventor to prove that he or she was in fact the first to invent, which is a requirement under U.S. law. Recall also that even one reference, whether in the prior art or in the knowledge of those with ordinary skill in the art, will be enough to deny patent protection. Thus, before filing a patent application, a business should undertake a prior art search of previously issued patents; published patent applications; advertisements, notices, and articles in trade or scholarly journals and similar publications; as well as other related sources available in the United States and abroad.

Once it is decided to proceed, the patent application should be filed as soon as possible. A qualified patent attorney will be invaluable in drafting the often-complex language that defines the claims and specifications that describe the invention in the patent application. Where patent protection is not available, a business should consider using copyright and trade secret as a means of protecting its intellectual property. Indeed, it may make sense to consider copyright protection even if the software is patentable. Likewise, a firm that is doing business in other countries should pursue patent protection there as well, if it is available. As the *State Street Bank* case reveals, a patent will not preclude an infringement claim by a competitor, or a claim of invalidity as a defense by a competitor against whom the patent is enforced, but a patent creates a rebuttable presumption of validity and enforceability. This also suggests that it is important for a business to be aware of the patents held by competitors in order to avoid infringement suits and become aware of prior art that may prevent the USPTO from issuing a patent due to obviousness.

If a competitor or any other person steps forward to challenge the software or business method patent, a patent attorney will be needed to defend the validity of patent at the USPTO or in court. If a business is sued for or threatened with a suit for patent infringement, it can continue to use, make, or sell the technology without permission, and then contest the validity of the patent in court, as did Barnes & Noble in the *Amazon.com* case. An alternative and more proactive strategy is to petition the USPTO to reexamine the patent at issue before an infringement claim is raised. When the USPTO conducts a reexamination procedure, it reconsiders the patentability of the invention or discovery in light of any prior art not revealed in the original examination process. If the USPTO determines that there is a substantial evidence that the invention is obvious or not novel in light of the new information, the patent will be invalidated and the invention can be used without threat of infringement. Finally, if a business licenses the rights of another's patented software or business method, it should be sure to include in the licensing agreement a warranty that the licensor actually owns the patent, as well as a promise to indemnify the business against any claims by third parties for infringement.

Endnotes

[1] See 35 U.S.C. §§ 101–103. The focus of this discussion is utility patents, though design patents may be issued for ornamental product shapes or designs.

[2] A purely aesthetic invention that is not functional may qualify for a design patent.

[3] Once a patent has expired, the invention passes into the public domain and it can be made, used, or sold by others without permission from the owner of the expired patent.

[4] As a defensive measure, the alleged infringer may argue that the patent is invalid and should have never been issued in the first place. If the patent is found to be invalid, then the suit will be dismissed, leaving the patent owner without a patent or a remedy.

[5] 21 U.S.T. 1583, T.I.A.S. No. 6295, 828 U.N.T.S. 305 (last revision entered into force Apr. 26, 1970).

[6] 28 U.S.T. 7645, T.I.A.S. No. 8733 (entered into force Jan. 24, 1978).

[7] 409 U.S. 63 (1972).

[8] *Id.* See also *Parker v. Flook*, 437 U.S. 584 (1978) (holding unpatentable a program used to compute a number used as an alarm number).

[9] 450 U.S. 175 (1981).

[10] *Id.*

[11] The Federal Circuit settled on what was known as the *Freeman-Walter-Abele* test to identify unpatentable claims involving mathematical algorithms. Under this test, the claims of a patent first must be analyzed to determine whether a mathematical algorithm is directly or indirectly cited. Next, if a mathematical algorithm is found, the claim as a whole is further analyzed to determine whether the algorithm is applied in any manner to physical elements or process steps, and if it is, it meets the standards of the Patent Act.

[12] 61 Fed. Reg. 7478 (Feb. 28, 1996).

[13] *Id.* In addition, the USPTO has issued standards that govern the patentability of computer icons used for a display screen. If such icons meet the highly technical requirements, they will qualify for a design patent. See USPTO, "Guidelines for the Examination of Design Patent Applications for Computer-Generated Icons," *U.S. Patent & Trademark Official Gazette*, April 16, 1996, http://www.uspto.gov/web/patents/guides.htm.

[14] 927 F.3d 1368 (fed. Cir. 1998).

[15] As discussed earlier in the text in relation to computer programs, State Street had relied on the so-called "mathematical algorithm exception," which was applied to deny patentability to inventions that involved mathematical algorithms that produced no practical utility.

[16] *Id.*

[17] *Id.*

[18] For a list and descriptions of these and other recently issued on-line business method patents, and a discussion of related litigation, see Hayes, D. L., "What the General Intellectual Property Practitioner Should Know About Patenting Business Methods," *Computer Lawyer*, Vol. 16, 1999, p. 3; Yoches , E. R., "Business-Method Patent Litigation," 2000, www.udayton.edu/~lawtech/papers/Chapter%2015.htm.

[19] 172 F.3d 1352 (Fed. Cir. 1999).

[20] *Id.*

[21] See Yoches, *supra* note 16.

[22] See *Amazon.com, Inc. v. Barnesandnoble.com, Inc.*, 73 F. Supp. 2d 1228 (W.D. Wash. 2000).

[23] See *Amazon.com, Inc. v. Barnesandnoble.com, Inc.*, No. 00-1109 (Fed. Cir. 2001).

[24] The USPTO's initiative to improve the process for examining business method patent applications is detailed in "United States Patent & Trademark Office White Paper on Automated Financial or Management Data Processing Methods (Business Methods)," March 29, 2000, www.uspto.gov/web/menu/busmethp/index.html.

[25] For a discussion of the field of potential prior art relating to business methods, see Merges, R. P., "As Many as Six Impossible Patents Before Breakfast: Property Rights for Business Concepts and Patent System Reform," *Berkeley Tech. L.J.*, Vol. 14, 1999, p. 577.

[26] Japanese Patent Office, "Examination of Business-Method Inventions," December 1999, www.jpo-miti.go.jp/infoe/treatment.htm.

[27] U.K. Patent Office, "Should Patents Be Granted for Computer Software or Ways of Doing Business?: The Government's Conclusions," March 2001, www.patent.gov.uk/about/concultations/conclusions.htm.

Appendix: How users access and use the Internet

Congress enacted the Communications Decency Act (CDA) in 1996 in an effort to regulate the obscene and indecent content on Web sites. The CDA was immediately challenged by the American Civil Liberties Union, and in the case of *Reno v. UCLA* [1], the United States Supreme Court ultimately struck down the CDA as an unconstitutional restraint on freedom of speech protected by the First Amendment to the United States Constitution. Before the case reached the Supreme Court, however, it was considered by a federal district court, which issued a detailed opinion that described in plain language how users access the Internet and the means by which they communicate while using it. It remains one of the best descriptions of the Internet in American law, and it is reproduced, in pertinent part, below [2].

How individuals access the Internet

12. Individuals have a wide variety of avenues to access cyberspace in general, and the Internet in particular. In terms of physical access, there are two common methods to establish an actual link to the Internet. First, one can use a computer or computer terminal that is directly (and usually permanently) connected to a computer network that is itself directly or indirectly connected to the Internet. Second, one can use a "personal computer" with a "modem" to connect over a telephone line to a larger computer or computer network that is itself directly or indirectly connected to the Internet. As detailed below, both direct and modem connections are made available to people by a wide variety of academic, governmental, or commercial entities.

13. Students, faculty, researchers, and others affiliated with the vast majority of colleges and universities in the United States can access the Internet through their educational institutions. Such access is often via direct connection using computers located in campus libraries, offices, or computer centers, or may be through telephone access using a modem from a student's or professor's campus or off-campus location. Some colleges and universities install "ports" or outlets for direct network connections in each dormitory room or provide access via computers located in common areas in dormitories. Such access enables students and professors to use information and content provided by the college or university itself, and to use the vast amount of research resources and other information available on the Internet worldwide.

14. Similarly, Internet resources and access are sufficiently important to many corporations and other employers that those employers link their office computer networks to the Internet and provide employees with direct or modem access to the office network (and thus to the Internet). Such access might be used by, for example, a corporation involved in scientific or medical research or manufacturing to enable corporate employees to exchange information and ideas with academic researchers in their fields.

15. Those who lack access to the Internet through their schools or employers still have a variety of ways they can access the Internet. Many

communities across the country have established "free-nets" or community networks to provide their citizens with a local link to the Internet (and to provide local-oriented content and discussion groups). The first such community network, the Cleveland Free-Net Community Computer System, was established in 1986, and free-nets now exist in scores of communities as diverse as Richmond, Virginia, Tallahassee, Florida, Seattle, Washington, and San Diego, California. Individuals typically can access free-nets at little or no cost via modem connection or by using computers available in community buildings. Free-nets are often operated by a local library, educational institution, or non-profit community group.

16. Individuals can also access the Internet through many local libraries. Libraries often offer patrons use of computers that are linked to the Internet. In addition, some libraries offer telephone modem access to the libraries' computers, which are themselves connected to the Internet. Increasingly, patrons now use library services and resources without ever physically entering the library itself. Libraries typically provide such direct or modem access at no cost to the individual user.

17. Individuals can also access the Internet by patronizing an increasing number of storefront "computer coffee shops," where customers—while they drink their coffee—can use computers provided by the shop to access the Internet. Such Internet access is typically provided by the shop for a small hourly fee.

18. Individuals can also access the Internet through commercial and non-commercial "Internet service providers" that typically offer modem telephone access to a computer or computer network linked to the Internet. Many such providers—including the members of plaintiff Commercial Internet Exchange Association—are commercial entities offering Internet access for a monthly or hourly fee. Some Internet service providers, however, are non-profit organizations that offer free or very low cost access to the Internet. For example, the International Internet Association offers free modem access to the Internet upon request. Also, a number of trade or other non-profit associations offer Internet access as a service to members.

19. Another common way for individuals to access the Internet is through one of the major national commercial "online services" such as America Online, CompuServe, the Microsoft Network, or Prodigy. These online services offer nationwide computer networks (so that subscribers can dial-in to a local telephone number), and the services provide extensive and well organized content within their own proprietary computer networks. In addition to allowing access to the extensive content available within each online service, the services also allow subscribers to link to the much larger resources of the Internet. Full access to the online service (including access to the Internet) can be obtained for modest monthly or hourly fees. The major commercial online services have almost twelve million individual subscribers across the United States.

20. In addition to using the national commercial online services, individuals can also access the Internet using some (but not all) of the thousands of local dial-in computer services, often called "bulletin board systems" or "BBSs." With an investment of as little as $2,000.00 and the cost of a telephone line, individuals, non-profit organizations, advocacy groups, and businesses can offer their own dial-in computer "bulletin board" service where friends, members, subscribers, or customers can exchange ideas and information. BBSs range from single computers with only one telephone line into the computer (allowing only one user at a time), to single computers with many telephone lines into the computer (allowing multiple simultaneous users), to multiple linked computers each servicing multiple dial-in telephone lines (allowing multiple simultaneous users). Some (but not all) of these BBS systems offer direct or indirect links to the Internet. Some BBS systems charge users a nominal fee for access, while many others are free to the individual users.

21. Although commercial access to the Internet is growing rapidly, many users of the Internet—such as college students and staff—do not individually pay for access (except to the extent, for example, that the cost of computer services is a component of college tuition). These and other Internet users can access the Internet without paying for such access with a credit card or other form of payment.

Methods to communicate over the Internet

22. Once one has access to the Internet, there are a wide variety of different methods of communication and information exchange over the network. These many methods of communication and information retrieval are constantly evolving and are therefore difficult to categorize concisely. The most common methods of communications on the Internet (as well as within the major online services) can be roughly grouped into six categories:

(1) one-to-one messaging (such as "e-mail"),

(2) one-to-many messaging (such as "listserv"),

(3) distributed message databases (such as "USENET newsgroups"),

(4) real time communication (such as "Internet Relay Chat"),

(5) real time remote computer utilization (such as "telnet"), and

(6) remote information retrieval (such as "ftp," "gopher," and the "World Wide Web").

Most of these methods of communication can be used to transmit text, data, computer programs, sound, visual images (i.e., pictures), and moving video images.

23. *One-to-one messaging.* One method of communication on the Internet is via electronic mail, or "e-mail," comparable in principle to sending a first class letter. One can address and transmit a message to one or more other people. E-mail on the Internet is not routed through a central control point, and can take many and varying paths to the recipients. Unlike postal mail, simple e-mail generally is not "sealed" or secure, and can be accessed or viewed on intermediate computers between the sender and recipient (unless the message is encrypted).

24. *One-to-many messaging.* The Internet also contains automatic mailing list services (such as "listservs"), [also referred to by witnesses as "mail exploders"] that allow communications about particular subjects of interest to a group of people. For example, people can subscribe to a "listserv" mailing list on a particular topic of interest to them. The subscriber

can submit messages on the topic to the listserv that are forwarded (via e-mail), either automatically or through a human moderator overseeing the listserv, to anyone who has subscribed to the mailing list. A recipient of such a message can reply to the message and have the reply also distributed to everyone on the mailing list. This service provides the capability to keep abreast of developments or events in a particular subject area. Most listserv-type mailing lists automatically forward all incoming messages to all mailing list subscribers. There are thousands of such mailing list services on the Internet, collectively with hundreds of thousands of subscribers. Users of "open" listservs typically can add or remove their names from the mailing list automatically, with no direct human involvement. Listservs may also be "closed," i.e., only allowing for one's acceptance into the listserv by a human moderator.

25. *Distributed message databases.* Similar in function to listservs—but quite different in how communications are transmitted—are distributed message databases such as "USENET newsgroups." User-sponsored newsgroups are among the most popular and widespread applications of Internet services, and cover all imaginable topics of interest to users. Like listservs, newsgroups are open discussions and exchanges on particular topics. Users, however, need not subscribe to the discussion mailing list in advance, but can instead access the database at any time. Some USENET newsgroups are "moderated" but most are open access. For the moderated newsgroups, all messages to the newsgroup are forwarded to one person who can screen them for relevance to the topics under discussion. USENET newsgroups are disseminated using ad hoc, peer to peer connections between approximately 200,000 computers (called USENET "servers") around the world. For unmoderated newsgroups, when an individual user with access to a USENET server posts a message to a newsgroup, the message is automatically forwarded to all adjacent USENET servers that furnish access to the newsgroup, and it is then propagated to the servers adjacent to those servers, etc. The messages are temporarily stored on each receiving server, where they are available for review and response by individual users. The messages are automatically and periodically purged from each system after a time to make room for new messages. Responses to messages, like the original messages, are automatically distributed to all other computers receiving the newsgroup or forwarded to a moderator in the case of a moderated newsgroup. The

dissemination of messages to USENET servers around the world is an automated process that does not require direct human intervention or review.

26. There are newsgroups on more than fifteen thousand different subjects. In 1994, approximately 70,000 messages were posted to newsgroups each day, and those messages were distributed to the approximately 190,000 computers or computer networks that participate in the USENET newsgroup system. Once the messages reach the approximately 190,000 receiving computers or computer networks, they are available to individual users of those computers or computer networks. Collectively, almost 100,000 new messages (or "articles") are posted to newsgroups each day.

27. *Real time communication.* In addition to transmitting messages that can be later read or accessed, individuals on the Internet can engage in an immediate dialog, in "real time," with other people on the Internet. In its simplest forms, "talk" allows one-to-one communications and "Internet Relay Chat" (or IRC) allows two or more to type messages to each other that almost immediately appear on the others' computer screens. IRC is analogous to a telephone party line, using a computer and keyboard rather than a telephone. With IRC, however, at any one time there are thousands of different party lines available, in which collectively tens of thousands of users are engaging in conversations on a huge range of subjects. Moreover, one can create a new party line to discuss a different topic at any time. Some IRC conversations are "moderated" or include "channel operators."

28. In addition, commercial online services such as America Online, CompuServe, the Microsoft Network, and Prodigy have their own "chat" systems allowing their members to converse.

29. *Real time remote computer utilization.* Another method to use information on the Internet is to access and control remote computers in "real time" using "telnet." For example, using telnet, a researcher at a university would be able to use the computing power of a supercomputer located at a different university. A student can use telnet to connect to a remote library to access the library's online card catalog program.

30. *Remote information retrieval.* The final major category of communication may be the most well known use of the Internet — the search for and retrieval of information located on remote computers. There are three primary methods to locate and retrieve information on the Internet.

31. A simple method uses "ftp" (or file transfer protocol) to list the names of computer files available on a remote computer, and to transfer one or more of those files to an individual's local computer.

32. Another approach uses a program and format named "gopher" to guide an individual's search through the resources available on a remote computer.

The World Wide Web

33. A third approach, and fast becoming the most well-known on the Internet, is the "World Wide Web." The Web utilizes a "hypertext" formatting language called hypertext markup language (HTML), and programs that "browse" the Web can display HTML documents containing text, images, sound, animation and moving video. Any HTML document can include links to other types of information or resources, so that while viewing an HTML document that, for example, describes resources available on the Internet, one can "click" using a computer mouse on the description of the resource and be immediately connected to the resource itself. Such "hyperlinks" allow information to be accessed and organized in very flexible ways, and allow people to locate and efficiently view related information even if the information is stored on numerous computers all around the world.

34. *Purpose.* The World Wide Web (W3C) was created to serve as the platform for a global, online store of knowledge, containing information from a diversity of sources and accessible to Internet users around the world. Though information on the Web is contained in individual computers, the fact that each of these computers is connected to the Internet through W3C protocols allows all of the information to become part of a single body of knowledge. It is currently the most advanced information system developed on the Internet, and embraces within its data model

most information in previous networked information systems such as ftp, gopher, wais, and Usenet.

35. *History.* W3C was originally developed at CERN, the European Particle Physics Laboratory, and was initially used to allow information sharing within internationally dispersed teams of researchers and engineers. Originally aimed at the High Energy Physics community, it has spread to other areas and attracted much interest in user support, resource recovery, and many other areas which depend on collaborative and information sharing. The Web has extended beyond the scientific and academic community to include communications by individuals, non-profit organizations, and businesses.

36. *Basic Operation.* The World Wide Web is a series of documents stored in different computers all over the Internet. Documents contain information stored in a variety of formats, including text, still images, sounds, and video. An essential element of the Web is that any document has an address (rather like a telephone number). Most Web documents contain "links." These are short sections of text or image which refer to another document. Typically the linked text is blue or underlined when displayed, and when selected by the user, the referenced document is automatically displayed, wherever in the world it actually is stored. Links for example are used to lead from overview documents to more detailed documents, from tables of contents to particular pages, but also as cross-references, footnotes, and new forms of information structure.

37. Many organizations now have "home pages" on the Web. These are documents which provide a set of links designed to represent the organization, and through links from the home page, guide the user directly or indirectly to information about or relevant to that organization.

38. As an example of the use of links, if these Findings were to be put on a World Wide Web site, its home page might contain links such as those:

(1) THE NATURE OF CYBERSPACE

(2) CREATION OF THE INTERNET AND THE DEVELOPMENT OF CYBERSPACE

(3) HOW PEOPLE ACCESS THE INTERNET

(4) METHODS TO COMMUNICATE OVER THE INTERNET

39. Each of these links takes the user of the site from the beginning of the Findings to the appropriate section within this Adjudication. Links may also take the user from the original Web site to another Web site on another computer connected to the Internet. These links from one computer to another, from one document to another across the Internet, are what unify the Web into a single body of knowledge, and what makes the Web unique. The Web was designed with a maximum target time to follow a link of one tenth of a second.

40. *Publishing.* The World Wide Web exists fundamentally as a platform through which people and organizations can communicate through shared information. When information is made available, it is said to be "published" on the Web. Publishing on the Web simply requires that the "publisher" has a computer connected to the Internet and that the computer is running W3C server software. The computer can be as simple as a small personal computer costing less than $1500 dollars or as complex as a multi-million dollar mainframe computer. Many Web publishers choose instead to lease disk storage space from someone else who has the necessary computer facilities, eliminating the need for actually owning any equipment oneself.

41. The Web, as a universe of network accessible information, contains a variety of documents prepared with quite varying degrees of care, from the hastily typed idea, to the professionally executed corporate profile. The power of the Web stems from the ability of a link to point to any document, regardless of its status or physical location.

42. Information to be published on the Web must also be formatted according to the rules of the Web standards. These standardized formats assure that all Web users who want to read the material will be able to view it. Web standards are sophisticated and flexible enough that they have grown to meet the publishing needs of many large corporations, banks, brokerage houses, newspapers and magazines which now publish "online" editions of their material, as well as government agencies, and even

courts, which use the Web to disseminate information to the public. At the same time, Web publishing is simple enough that thousands of individual users and small community organizations are using the Web to publish their own personal "home pages," the equivalent of individualized newsletters about that person or organization, which are available to everyone on the Web.

43. Web publishers have a choice to make their Web sites open to the general pool of all Internet users, or close them, thus making the information accessible only to those with advance authorization. Many publishers choose to keep their sites open to all in order to give their information the widest potential audience. In the event that the publishers choose to maintain restrictions on access, this may be accomplished by assigning specific user names and passwords as a prerequisite to access to the site. Or, in the case of Web sites maintained for internal use of one organization, access will only be allowed from other computers within that organization's local network.

44. *Searching the Web.* A variety of systems have developed that allow users of the Web to search particular information among all of the public sites that are part of the Web. Services such as Yahoo, Magellan, Altavista, Webcrawler, and Lycos are all services known as "search engines" which allow users to search for Web sites that contain certain categories of information, or to search for key words. For example, a Web user looking for the text of Supreme Court opinions would type the words "Supreme Court" into a search engine, and then be presented with a list of World Wide Web sites that contain Supreme Court information. This list would actually be a series of links to those sites. Having searched out a number of sites that might contain the desired information, the user would then follow individual links, browsing through the information on each site, until the desired material is found. For many content providers on the Web, the ability to be found by these search engines is very important.

45. *Common standards.* The Web links together disparate information on an ever-growing number of Internet-linked computers by setting common information storage formats (HTML) and a common language for the exchange of Web documents (HTTP). Although the information itself may be in many different formats, and stored on computers which are

not otherwise compatible, the basic Web standards provide a basic set of standards which allow communication and exchange of information. Despite the fact that many types of computers are used on the Web, and the fact that many of these machines are otherwise incompatible, those who "publish" information on the Web are able to communicate with those who seek to access information with little difficulty because of these basic technical standards.

46. *A distributed system with no centralized control.* Running on tens of thousands of individual computers on the Internet, the Web is what is known as a distributed system. The Web was designed so that organizations with computers containing information can become part of the Web simply by attaching their computers to the Internet and running appropriate World Wide Web software. No single organization controls any membership in the Web, nor is there any single centralized point from which individual Web sites or services can be blocked from the Web. From a user's perspective, it may appear to be a single, integrated system, but in reality it has no centralized control point.

47. *Contrast to closed databases.* The Web's open, distributed, decentralized nature stands in sharp contrast to most information systems that have come before it. Private information services such as Westlaw, Lexis/Nexis, and Dialog, have contained large storehouses of knowledge, and can be accessed from the Internet with the appropriate passwords and access software. However, these databases are not linked together into a single whole, as is the World Wide Web.

48. *Success of the Web in research, education, and political activities.* The World Wide Web has become so popular because of its open, distributed, and easy-to-use nature. Rather than requiring those who seek information to purchase new software or hardware, and to learn a new kind of system for each new database of information they seek to access, the Web environment makes it easy for users to jump from one set of information to another. By the same token, the open nature of the Web makes it easy for publishers to reach their intended audiences without having to know in advance what kind of computer each potential reader has, and what kind of software they will be using.

Endnotes

[1] 117 S.Ct. 2329 (1997).

[2] *ACLU v. Reno*, 929 F. Supp. 824, 830–849 (E.D. Pa. 1998) (citations omitted).

Glossary

agency relationship An agency relationship exists when one person (the agent) is authorized by another person (the principal) to act on behalf of and under the control of the principal.

algorithm A step-by-step procedure, method, or set of instructions designed to produce a specific result or solve a specific problem.

appeal A request brought by the losing party to an appellate court that the decision of a lower court be reviewed.

ARPANET The Advanced Research Projects Agency Network was the forerunner of the Internet and was created in 1969 by the United States Defense Advanced Research Projects Agency (DARPA).

bit A bit, or binary digit, is the digit 0 or 1 used to encode computer data.

browser A computer program used to access, display, and interact with information and files available on the Internet.

bulletin board system A bulletin board system (BBS) is a dial-in computer system that allows users to meet on-line, carry on discussions, upload and download files, and make announcements.

byte A set or string of 8 bits representing a single character.

case A legal dispute resolved by a court.

chatroom Software that allows two or more users to engage in real-time dialog by typing messages that are instantly sent and that appear on a computer screen display.

civil law The rules of law that govern relations and lawsuits between private parties.

claim The basis in law that supports a plaintiff's request for relief.

computer crime Computer crime is any conduct that employs information technology to accomplish an illegal purpose (also referred to as *cybercrime*).

computer network A computer network is a group of computers linked to one another so that they can share files and exchange messages.

contract A legally enforceable agreement or set of mutual promises.

cookie A piece of information sent by a server to a browser that the browser software saves on the user's computer and later sends back to the server whenever the browser makes additional requests from the server. A cookie might be used to gather information about a user, or they might contain information such as login or registration information, user preferences, or other similar information.

copyright A copyright is a grant of exclusive rights to authors of certain types of creative *works*, whether published or unpublished, lasting for the author's life plus an additional 70 years after his or her death. To be protected under the Copyright Act, these must be original works of authorship fixed in any tangible medium of expression from which they can be perceived, reproduced, or otherwise communicated either directly or with the aid of a machine or device.

copyright infringement When anyone other than the copyright owner, or the lawful transferee, of a copyright exercises any of the exclusive rights afforded by a copyright, there is an infringement of the copyright and the owner may sue for damages. Infringement need not be intentional and may be done subconsciously or innocently.

court A body of the judicial branch of the state or federal government that resolves disputes. The initial court that hears a case may be referred to as a lower, trial, or district court, and the court that decides a case on appeal may be referred to as an appellate court or court of appeals.

crime An act or public wrong prohibited and punishable by the government.

criminal law The rules of law that define crimes that will be prosecuted by the government.

cyberstalking A computer crime involving on-line threats or harassment directed against another.

cyberspace A term first used by author William Gibson in his novel, *Neuromancer*, now used to describe the entirety of information and technologies available on the Internet.

damages An award of money recovered by a plaintiff who has won a civil lawsuit.

data Electronically stored information, including facts, concepts, instructions, and programs.

database A collection of electronic information stored and accessed on a computer.

defendant The party who is sued in a civil case or who is prosecuted in a criminal case.

defense A rule of law that permits a defendant to avoid liability even if the plaintiff proves his or her claim.

digital encryption Using a computer program, a mathematical equation, known as an encryption algorithm, encodes and converts a plaintext message using a key into unintelligible ciphertext.

digital signature A digital signature, which can be generated using a digital encryption program, functions as a seal of verification that the message has not been modified without the sender's authorization.

domain name A domain name functions as an alphanumeric address for an Internet Web site, allowing consumers to identify and locate particular businesses in much the same way as a street address or telephone number.

domain name registrar A private firm appointed by ICANN to assign and register domain names.

dual-use technology A dual-use technology is one that has both military and civilian uses.

e-mail E-mail, or electronic mail, are messages sent automatically by one person to others using a computer.

fair use A defense to copyright and trademark infringement claims when a court deems that the infringing use should not subject the defendant to liability.

FAQ An acronym for frequently asked questions, which are text files that list and answer the most common questions on a particular subject.

file The physical space on which data is stored on a computer.

firewall A system or combination of hardware and software that creates a boundary that separates a LAN into two or more parts for security purposes.

First Amendment The initial amendment to the United States Constitution guaranteeing certain fundamental rights, including freedom of speech.

forum A court or jurisdiction in which a lawsuit is resolved.

framing Framing allows the viewer to click on a hyperlink, which then displays within a bordered frame on the Web site being viewed, material that is located on another Web site under another URL.

FTP File transfer protocol is a standard protocol used for transferring files from one computer to another on the Internet.

hacking Hacking occurs when a computer is the target of a crime by a perpetrator who utilizes the computer to gain access to data or programs stored on the computer without authorization. The purpose is to steal information stored on the system, to gain control of the system, or to sabotage or alter the integrity of stored data.

hardware The physical elements of equipment comprising a computer, including the central processing unit, printer, monitor, keyboard, and mouse.

home page The Web page of a business, organization, or person that a browser is set to open to when it starts running.

HTML Hypertext markup language is the main computer programming language used to create sites on the World Wide Web for display by an Internet browser such as Netscape Communicator or Microsoft Explorer. The HTML coding is not visible to the viewer; rather, the text and graphical images and the manner in which they have been arranged by the code is what appears when a Web page is displayed.

HTTP Hypertext transfer protocol is the protocol used to transmit files across the Internet and on the World Wide Web.

hypertext linking Hypertext links, or links or hyperlinks, allow Web site owners to connect their sites to sites containing related information located elsewhere. The links are constructed using HTML and may appear as underlined text or graphical images.

ICANN The Internet Corporation for Assigned Names and Numbers is a private nonprofit corporation assumed responsibility for designating registrars of domain names.

information technology The computer hardware and software used to access, create, manipulate, send, retrieve, and store data, and to perform related functions.

injunction A remedy whereby a court orders a defendant to perform an act or desist from an action.

intellectual property Exclusive rights of ownership and use over certain creations or inventions granted or recognized by the government and protected by law. Patents, copyrights, trademarks, and trade secrets are forms of intellectual property.

Internet The Internet is an enormous network that interconnects numerous smaller groups of interlinked computer networks using the TCP/IP protocol standard, and that links people, institutions, businesses, and governments around the world in a decentralized medium of international communications using various common data transfer protocols.

intranet An intranet is private network of interlinked computer networks within an organization for use only by its members.

invasion of privacy One is liable for invasion of privacy when he or she unreasonably intrudes upon an area or the affairs of another person in which that person has a reasonable expectation of privacy.

ISP An Internet service provider is an entity that provides access to the Internet to users, often in exchange for a fee, though not-for-profit institutions such as universities and government agencies may provide access as well.

judgment A final resolution of a lawsuit by a court.

jurisdiction Jurisdiction is the authority of a court to exercise its authority over the parties involved in the dispute and to issue a judgment that is binding on the parties.

LAN A LAN is an acronym for local area naetwork, which is a computer network limited to the local geographic area.

listserv A mailing list system, usually automated, that allows a subscriber to send email to one address, where it is then copied and sent to all of the other subscribers to the list, allowing subscribers to participate in discussions of various topics.

liability The potential that an action or failure to act will lead to a lawsuit and a court determination that another is entitled to relief.

litigation A lawsuit or the process of suing and deciding a lawsuit.

log in/off The process by which a user gains access to (log in) or terminates use of (log off) a computer system.

metatag Metatags are used to designate words that are written in HTML and identifiable to search engines, some of which are not visible to the eye. Search engines index certain selected keywords appearing in the

HTML version of the website document and use the first words found in the document as an abstract to direct a consumer to the site.

modem A modem, or modulator/demodulator, is a device that allows a computer to communicate with other computers by transmitting and receiving information over telephone lines or satellites.

newsgroup An electronic discussion group on USENET allowing users to post and read messages posted by other users.

node Any computer connected to a network.

NSF An acronym for the National Science Foundation, which played a major role in creating the Internet and the domain name registration system.

object code The version of a computer program in language that can be read and executed directly by the computer without translation.

operating system A complex computer program that controls the basic functioning of a computer.

on-line A user's ability to access and interact with a computer and a network.

password A password is an alphanumeric code used to gain access to a locked computer system.

patent A patent is a grant issued by the federal government that gives an inventor the right to exclude all others from making, using, or selling his or her invention within the United States, its territories, and possessions for a period of 20 years.

patent infringement A patent owner may bring an infringement action in a federal court against anyone who uses, makes, or sells his or her invention without permission.

preliminary injunction A form of relief granted by a court when it finds that the plaintiff will likely win the lawsuit but will suffer irreparable injury unless the defendant's conduct is immediately halted.

protocol A set or procedures, conventions, or rules that determine how a computer communicates with other computers or networks.

punitive damages Punitive damages, also referred to as exemplary damages, are additional money damages above actual loss suffered that may be imposed as a punishment for malicious or willful misappropriation or misconduct.

RAM Random access memory is the internal memory of a computer.

regulation A rule of law created and issued by a governmental administrative or regulatory body.

relief A judicial award of damages, an injunction, or other compensation to a plaintiff based on a determination that a right has been violated by the defendant.

remedy The type of relief appropriate to enforce a right.

respondeat superior Under the doctrine of respondeat superior, which means, "let the master answer," a principal-employer is liable for the unlawful acts of an agent-employee when he or she commits the acts with the scope of his or her employment. This rule is one of vicarious liability for the employer because the liability is premised on his or her relationship with the employee rather than on any fault on his or her part.

right An interest or entitlement created by and protected by law.

ROM Read only memory is a semiconductor chip containing a permanently stored program or data when the computer is manufactured.

screen display The audiovisual appearance of a program that is sometimes also referred to as a graphical user interface.

search engine A computer program, sometimes referred to as a spider or crawler, that allows users to search for information stored on the Internet using key words and phrases. The program indexes the retrieved information, data, or URLs.

server A computer, storage device, or program that provides on-line content and service to users.

software A computer program.

source code The set of instructions, expressed in a programming language understandable by trained persons, to a computer for carrying out the various tasks performed by a program.

spam Unsolicited or inappropriate e-mail sent to a large number of recipients on a mailing list.

spreadsheet program A computer program that organizes data in a matrix of rows and columns.

statute A law in the form or legislation enacted by a Congress or a state legislature and signed by the president or governor.

SYSOP A SYSOP, or system operator, is a person responsible for the physical operations of a computer system or network.

TCP/IP The system of protocols or rules known as the transmission control protocol (TCP) and the Internet protocol (IP) that is the standard for linking to and sharing information on the Internet.

terminal The computer hardware device that allows a user, by way of a keyboard, to send commands to a computer, which may be located elsewhere, and then view information on a display screen.

tort Wrongful or harmful conduct against another's person or property that may lead to a civil lawsuit for damages or other relief.

trade secret Any information, including a formula, pattern, compilation, program, device, method, technique, or process that derives independent economic value, actual or potential, from not being generally known to, and not being readily ascertainable by proper means by, other persons who can obtain economic value from its disclosure or use; and is the subject of efforts that are reasonable under the circumstances to maintain secrecy.

trade secret misappropriation Trade secret misappropriation occurs when the secret is disclosed by someone in violation of a contractual duty to maintain its confidentiality, such as when an employee or partner breaches a confidentiality agreement, or when the secret is obtained by another through improper means, such when a competitor gains possession through theft or industrial espionage.

trademark A trademark is any word, name, symbol, or device, or any combination thereof used to identify and distinguish goods from those manufactured or sold by others and to indicate the source of the goods.

trademark dilution Dilution occurs when, through the use of a similar or identical trademark, a strong and well-known registered trademark is tarnished or weakened as a means of identifying and distinguishing a particular product or service.

trademark infringement Infringement occurs when the use of a mark by one person creates a "likelihood of confusion" with the trademark of another in the minds of consumers.

URL A uniform resource locator is a Web site address and part of the standard address system of any Web site available on the Internet and the World Wide Web through a browser. Examples: http://www.artech-house.com or ftp://news.currentevents.usa.

USENET A system of discussion groups, bulletin board services, and newsgroups storing all of the comments posted in topical categories to be shared by users from all over the world.

USPTO An acronym for the United States Patent and Trademark Office, which is the federal agency that issues patents and trademarks.

virus An unsolicited computer program that attaches itself or "infects" the computer's operating system that can cause damage to the computer system, destroy or distort stored data, or cause other malfunctions (also referred to as a "worm").

Web page A computer data file that appears on or within a Web site.

Web site A collection of related, interactive documents on the Internet that share a common domain name or Internet address.

World Wide Web The World Wide Web, or WWW, is sometimes used to refer to the Internet, but is in fact the entire group of servers that allow users to search for and retrieve information stored in text, graphic, sound, and other files on other computers.

About the Author

Kurt M. Saunders is an assistant professor of business law at California State University, Northridge. He is a native of Pittsburgh, Pennsylvania, and graduated from Carnegie Mellon University with a B.S. in economics. He received his J.D. from the University of Pittsburgh and his LL.M. in intellectual property law from the George Washington University Law School, Washington, D.C. He practiced law in Pennsylvania, where he served as a jury commissioner before accepting his current teaching appointment. Mr. Saunders remains an active member of the Pennsylvania Bar, and currently teaches, conducts research, and consults in the areas of Internet law, intellectual property law, and antitrust law. In addition, he is a member of the American Intellectual Property Law Association, Internet Society, Computer Law Association, Pennsylvania Bar Association, and the Association of Practical and Professional Ethics.

Index

Recent Titles in the Artech House Telecommunications Library

Vinton G. Cerf, Senior Series Editor

Access Networks: Technology and V5 Interfacing, Alex Gillespie

Achieving Global Information Networking, Eve L. Varma, Thierry Stephant, et al.

Advanced High-Frequency Radio Communications, Eric E. Johnson, Robert I. Desourdis, Jr., et al.

ATM Switches, Edwin R. Coover

ATM Switching Systems, Thomas M. Chen and Stephen S. Liu

Broadband Access Technology, Interfaces, and Management, Alex Gillespie

Broadband Networking: ATM, SDH, and SONET, Mike Sexton and Andy Reid

Broadband Telecommunications Technology, Second Edition, Byeong Lee, Minho Kang, and Jonghee Lee

The Business Case for Web-Based Training, Tammy Whalen and David Wright

Communication and Computing for Distributed Multimedia Systems, Guojun Lu

Communications Technology Guide for Business, Richard Downey, Seán Boland, and Phillip Walsh

Community Networks: Lessons from Blacksburg, Virginia, Second Edition, Andrew M. Cohill and Andrea Kavanaugh, editors

Component-Based Network System Engineering, Mark Norris, Rob Davis, and Alan Pengelly

Computer Telephony Integration, Second Edition, Rob Walters

Desktop Encyclopedia of the Internet, Nathan J. Muller

Digital Modulation Techniques, Fuqin Xiong

E-Commerce Systems Architecture and Applications, Wasim E. Rajput

Error-Control Block Codes for Communications Engineers, L. H. Charles Lee

FAX: Facsimile Technology and Systems, Third Edition, Kenneth R. McConnell, Dennis Bodson, and Stephen Urban

Fundamentals of Network Security, John E. Canavan

Guide to ATM Systems and Technology, Mohammad A. Rahman

A Guide to the TCP/IP Protocol Suite, Floyd Wilder

Information Superhighways Revisited: The Economics of Multimedia, Bruce Egan

Internet E-mail: Protocols, Standards, and Implementation, Lawrence Hughes

Introduction to Telecommunications Network Engineering, Tarmo Anttalainen

Introduction to Telephones and Telephone Systems, Third Edition, A. Michael Noll

An Introduction to U.S. Telecommunications Law, Second Edition Charles H. Kennedy

IP Convergence: The Next Revolution in Telecommunications, Nathan J. Muller

The Law and Regulation of Telecommunications Carriers, Henk Brands and Evan T. Leo

Managing Internet-Driven Change in International Telecommunications, Rob Frieden

Marketing Telecommunications Services: New Approaches for a Changing Environment, Karen G. Strouse

Multimedia Communications Networks: Technologies and Services, Mallikarjun Tatipamula and Bhumip Khashnabish, editors

Performance Evaluation of Communication Networks, Gary N. Higginbottom

Performance of TCP/IP over ATM Networks, Mahbub Hassan and Mohammed Atiquzzaman

Practical Guide for Implementing Secure Intranets and Extranets, Kaustubh M. Phaltankar

Practical Internet Law for Business, Kurt M. Saunders

Practical Multiservice LANs: ATM and RF Broadband, Ernest O. Tunmann

Principles of Modern Communications Technology, A. Michael Noll

Protocol Management in Computer Networking, Philippe Byrnes

Pulse Code Modulation Systems Design, William N. Waggener

Service Level Management for Enterprise Networks, Lundy Lewis

SIP: Understanding the Session Initiation Protocol, Alan B. Johnston

Smart Card Security and Applications, Second Edition, Mike Hendry

SNMP-Based ATM Network Management, Heng Pan

Strategic Management in Telecommunications, James K. Shaw

Strategies for Success in the New Telecommunications Marketplace, Karen G. Strouse

Successful Business Strategies Using Telecommunications Services, Martin F. Bartholomew

Telecommunications Department Management, Robert A. Gable

Telecommunications Deregulation and the Information Economy, Second Edition, James K. Shaw

Telephone Switching Systems, Richard A. Thompson

Understanding Modern Telecommunications and the Information Superhighway, John G. Nellist and Elliott M. Gilbert

Understanding Networking Technology: Concepts, Terms, and Trends, Second Edition, Mark Norris

Videoconferencing and Videotelephony: Technology and Standards, Second Edition, Richard Schaphorst

Visual Telephony, Edward A. Daly and Kathleen J. Hansell

Wide-Area Data Network Performance Engineering,
Robert G. Cole and Ravi Ramaswamy

Winning Telco Customers Using Marketing Databases,
Rob Mattison

World-Class Telecommunications Service Development,
Ellen P. Ward

For further information on these and other Artech House titles, including previously considered out-of-print books now available through our In-Print-Forever® (IPF®) program, contact:

Artech House
685 Canton Street
Norwood, MA 02062
Phone: 781-769-9750
Fax: 781-769-6334
e-mail: artech@artechhouse.com

Artech House
46 Gillingham Street
London SW1V 1AH UK
Phone: +44 (0)20 7596-8750
Fax: +44 (0)20 7630-0166
e-mail: artech-uk@artechhouse.com

Find us on the World Wide Web at:
www.artechhouse.com